LIVING THE CHRISTIAN STORY

Living the Christian Story

The Good News in Worship and Daily Life

Sister Mary Jean Manninen, CSM

William B. Eerdmans Publishing Company
Grand Rapids, Michigan / Cambridge, U.K.

© 2000 Wm. B. Eerdmans Publishing Co.
255 Jefferson Ave. S.E., Grand Rapids, Michigan 49503 /
P.O. Box 163, Cambridge CB3 9PU U.K.

Printed in the United States of America

05   04 03 02 01 00   7 6 5 4 3 2 1

Library of Congress Cataloging-in-Publication Data

Manninen, Mary Jean.
   Living the Christian story / Mary Jean Manninen.
      p.   cm.
   Includes bibliographical references.
   ISBN 0-8028-4706-4 (pbk.: alk. paper)
    1. Christian life — Anglican authors.   2. Monastic and religious life.
    I. Title.
BV4501.2 .M3375 2000
248 — dc21   99-049031

Contents

Preface

The essays in this volume deal with a variety of topics in the fields of spirituality, biblical studies, liturgics, and the Christian life, and especially in the loosely defined area where all of these fields interact. The overall thread of the collection is defined by the opening chapter, "Christian Remembering."

This book owes its origin immediately to an invitation from Mr. David Mills to contribute to his series called "Books That Form Souls," which was published in *The Evangelical Catholic* in 1995. This exercise involved selecting no more than eight books, not counting the Bible, that had been especially formative in one's spiritual growth, and explaining why. Composing this piece was a challenging exercise. The point was, first, to limit the list to eight, and second, to be honest and list the really "formative" books, not the "right" ones or one's present-day favorites.

Seeing the result in cold print, next to other people's versions, was an eye-opening experience. Each of us has been shaped so largely by the minds and hearts of others: "What have I that I have not received?" Yet our personalities and thoughts are tremendously varied. Some books and authors, especially C. S. Lewis, were cited repeatedly and were more or less the "expected" ones. But the others ranged from Plato to modern science fiction. It seemed that others besides myself had been formed by a remarkable variety of ideas expressed in many different ways — theology, fiction, and poetry, as well as directly "devotional" or "instructive" writing.

This double insight into our interdependence and our difference seems to focus in the idea of "story." When I set out to tell "my story," it turns out to be not "my story" at all, in any private sense. It is the story of my relation with others and, as a Christian, ultimately with the Gospel and with God. Therefore it is my little piece of the one great Story. Each person's story fits into the one whole and also reflects in a unique way the themes of that one whole. In one sense, nothing and no one is original, and yet, in another sense, each of us is profoundly so.

The chapters that follow reflect on the Christian story and its manifestations in various ways. The theological perspective is one thoroughly committed to the Anglican[1] understanding of Christianity and holding to the faith of the Scriptures and creeds — what C. S. Lewis called "mere Christianity." There is no attempt to cover the whole of either the Christian Gospel or the monastic expression of it; in particular, there is no direct treatment of contemplative prayer.

The remote origin of these essays is forty years of living the monastic life in community, praying, working, studying, being family with my sisters, and above all being constantly steeped in the Divine Office and the Scriptures. This makes it almost impossible to identify or acknowledge the sources of many of the ideas used here, though I have tried to document specific references as fully as possible. Scripture quotations are generally from the Revised Standard Version.

Thanks for the formation and support I have received are due first to my sisters of the Community of St. Mary,[2] both those living

1. The Anglican Communion is the worldwide fellowship of churches (one of them the Episcopal Church in the United States) that are rooted in the tradition of the Church of England and are in communion with the See of Canterbury. An Anglican is a member of one of these churches; an Episcopalian is an American Anglican. Both terms are used in this book, but "Anglican" is preferred because it has a wider reference.

2. The Community of St. Mary, a monastic community for women in the Episcopal Church, was founded in New York City in 1865.

and many now departed. Thanks are also due to others who have contributed to shaping these ideas, especially the readers of the community's newsletter, *St. Mary's Messenger,* the participants in several retreats and "Benedictine workshops," and the young men and women of St. Michael's Conference, an Anglican teaching conference that meets each August near Boston.

Most of this material was first written for *St. Mary's Messenger* or for various teaching purposes. Some sections have been extensively recast, while others remain in their original form and style. "Honeycombs and Bible Critics" appeared in *The Evangelical Catholic* in 1994.

In community we have "all things common," and I do not know exactly where my ideas end and those of others begin. All the mistakes in fact or judgment, however, are mine, and I alone am responsible for any interpretations and opinions expressed in these pages.

Sister Mary Jean (Manninen), CSM
St. Mary's Convent
Peekskill, New York

I Christian Remembering

S uppose that your friend Meg, agnostic and innocent of any religious upbringing whatever, begins to inquire about the Christian faith. There are several ways you might respond. Perhaps a good place to begin would be to introduce her to Christians at worship. Suppose that you invite her to church with you, perhaps best of all to a great service like the Easter Vigil. Of course, she will need some preparation beforehand. You will want to give her some idea not only of what happens in this service but of what it means in terms of Christian faith and life.

The Great Vigil of Easter, recently restored in the Episcopal Church and other liturgical churches after a lapse of some centuries in the West, presents very dramatically the main features of the Christian story. It shows in full what the ordinary Sunday Eucharist summarizes on a much smaller scale. On the Saturday night that begins Easter, the Christian community gathers outdoors or in a darkened church while the deacon sings a quite remarkable and very ancient proclamation:

This is the night, when you brought our fathers, the children of Israel, out of bondage in Egypt, and led them through the Red Sea on dry land. This is the night, when all who believe in Christ are delivered from the gloom of sin, and are restored to grace and ho-

1

liness of life. This is the night, when Christ broke the bonds of death and hell, and rose victorious from the grave.[1]

Then several Old Testament lessons are read — nine when the service is used in full. These tell the whole biblical story from the Creation in Genesis, through the Exodus of Israel from Egypt and the crossing of the Red Sea, to the prophecies of the final restoration. Then the service moves to the administration of Christian Baptism, the Resurrection Gospel, and the Easter Eucharist.

This is the night. What do we mean, *this?* The Exodus from Egypt and the Resurrection of Christ are historic events long in the past. (Some would deny them even that historic reality, but that is another discussion.) What do they have to do with an American congregation at the threshold of the twenty-first century? What sort of present tense is this? And why these particular events?

An answer to these questions involves three outstanding and unmistakable characteristics of the Christian faith, which are made vivid and dramatic in liturgy:

- It is first of all a Story, a Story as long as time and as wide as human life, and a Story into which we are invited to enter. The Story in a nutshell is that God made man and gave him freedom, that man rebelled and misused that freedom, and that God has marvelously and at great cost restored man to his original status as the child of God.
- The Story is something *given,* recounting the mighty acts in history of a personal God. The worshipers are responding to Someone; their attention is directed toward the Author of the Story, the mysterious Other. They are looking toward the transcendent, not contemplating themselves or each other.
- This Story deals with a community, not primarily with individuals, and we experience it first of all in community.

---

1. The *Exsultet,* from *The Book of Common Prayer* (New York: Oxford University Press, 1979), p. 287.

*   *   *

One of the outstanding features of Christian faith is its emphasis upon *history*, upon the biblical story, upon narratives of one particular desert tribe and one particular Jewish teacher. To the outsider, and often to the questioning adolescent, this historicity has long presented a problem. "What can one man who lived two thousand years ago, in a backward country and another culture, have to do with *me?*" This questioning is accentuated today by the spread of a worldview that denies or ignores the historical altogether and finds it difficult to look beyond the immediate. We live today in a culture that, as Robert Jenson has said, has "lost its Story" and depends instead on a collage of unrelated sound bites.[2]

But the Christian tradition still has something to say in this rootless culture. It tells us that losing or denying our history means losing part of our identity, and that we can avoid this loss. Christianity offers even postmodern man a way back to his roots and his Story, and so offers a way into a far larger universe than the one called Now.

Acknowledging and recalling our history means recalling *all* of it. It is so easy to rewrite our past, to gloss over or deny our faults and failures, to magnify our own image. But both modern psychology and historic Christian wisdom teach us that this is self-defeating. The way to growth is to face truth and to come to terms with it. A full confession of past sin is one of the first steps in a serious Christian life. This is precisely the approach of the Scriptures to the history of the people of God. One might expect a community's own version of its history to glorify its past, its founders, and its leaders, but the Bible does not do this. It records instead the constant failures of the chosen people to live up to their calling. The prophets repeatedly denounce Israel for her faithlessness. The Old Testament tells us that David sinned greatly in killing Uriah and taking Bathsheba, and that he subsequently repented. The Gospel tells us that Peter denied the Lord and was restored to fellowship only after

---

2. Robert W. Jenson, "How the World Lost Its Story," *First Things* 36 (October 1993): 19-24.

he had "wept bitterly." The Bible does not glorify anyone but God, who alone is good and who alone can restore his erring children. The human story is told with all of its darkness as well as its light: that is why the biblical story is, as Isaiah said in another context, "as deep as Sheol and as high as heaven."

Christian liturgy brings together a number of themes, or dimensions, that can be shown to be interdependent. These themes can be called briefly *Scripture, community,* and *personal faith.* In liturgy all of these themes come together, enriching and illuminating each other. Scripture belongs in a liturgical, communal setting; the liturgy is formed largely from Scripture; personal faith flourishes best when grounded in community. These three themes are enhanced by a fourth, the *monastic* or Benedictine theme. The monastic life seeks corporate and individual growth in prayer and holiness, in community, in worship, and in the absorption of the truths of Scripture. Not only those who are called to the full-time monastic life but also many others who share in their tradition live out the constant interweaving of these themes.

Christianity treats its history both as solidly real in the past and as living and dynamic in the present, as the action of a living and personal God. Like our Jewish forebears, we encounter God by remembering and retelling his acts in time, in our own history. By recalling, retelling the story of the Creation, the Exodus, and the Resurrection in the Easter Vigil, we enter into a "sacred time" in which all of these events and our present worship are part of the same drama. We transcend the categories of "past" and "present" and become ourselves participants in the events we recall: *this* is the night. It is because of our experience of God's acts in the past that we recognize him at work in the present and look with confidence to his acts in the future.

This sense of history, of time as beginning somewhere and going somewhere, distinguishes the Judeo-Christian tradition from other worldviews. If the biblical view of history is as an arrow, a line with a direction (a vector), the view that may be loosely called Hindu sees history as cyclical. Some modern views would go further, seeing all events as random and unconnected, denying any meaning to either history or causality. However, in the biblical view the line, the sequence of events, is both real and unique, but it is not the whole of reality. From a vantage point above the line, from the viewpoint of "sacred time," we can, so to speak, rise above "time" and consider all its events as present in another dimension. The old book *Flatland* imagined a world of only two dimensions. Its inhabitants, characters like Square and Triangle, knew one another only edge-on; their first view of one another and of their flat world from above came as a tremendous shock.[3] Sacred time, Christian liturgical time, works in a somewhat similar way, acknowledging history as real and yet viewing it from a wider perspective. Saint Augustine taught that time is only our creaturely way of seeing reality; God created time as part of his creation of the world. In eternity, in God's sight, everything is present — or, better, simply Is.[4] Perhaps Albert Einstein's concept of time as a "fourth dimension" points to a similar idea in a twentieth-century idiom.

The reality of history has a corollary in the reality and importance of individual events. The "scandal of particularity," the idea that God could choose one people over another, and above all that the life, death, and resurrection of one Man could be the turning point of all history, offends many. It is easier to believe that all events are somehow "equal." But the point of this view of history is that events are not random, repeated, statistical, like molecules in a gas. Each is single and unrepeatable. Each event and each person has a unique place in the mind of God. This thought is today counterintuitive and countercultural, and for just that reason has great power. The Gospel calls each of us to lose himself and his "individuality" by entering into a larger Story. That call paradoxically also offers each of us a unique and irreplaceable role and an infinite value. As I enter into the Story of the people, so my own story becomes a part of its latest chapter in time and of its wholeness in eternity.

Just as Christian faith weaves past and present into a unity, so

3. *Flatland*, by Edwin Abbott, was first published in 1884. A recent edition, with a foreword by Isaac Asimov, was brought out by Harper & Row (Perennial Library) in 1984.

4. Augustine, *Confessions*, trans. and ed. John K. Ryan (Garden City, N.Y.: Doubleday–Image Books, 1960), 11:11, 14; pp. 285, 287.

it overcomes the division between "corporate" and "individual" lives of faith. We worship as a community, recalling the history of God's dealings with his people as a community, a *Qahal*, an *ecclesia*. (Both of these terms mean "a called-out assembly.") Yet it is in this corporate recalling that each of us can also find a particular, unique, and personal identity. The story of the Exodus, and then the story of Christ's death and resurrection, become also *my own* story. This shift in scales, this individual re-enactment, has modern parallels in other fields. It suggests the pattern found in fractal mathematics, where the same figures are repeated on ever larger or smaller scales. It also suggests the biologist's old tag, "Ontogeny recapitulates phylogeny" — in other words, the development of the individual parallels the development of the species. (An example of this would be that early mammalian embryos have gills.) The converse of this principle is also true. I can find my true identity, my true name, only by sharing in the life of the community, the people of God, and taking my proper place there.

*   *   *

Since as Christians we are grounded in history, we must *remember*. Much of Christian faith and worship involves remembering and retelling the story of God's mighty deeds, the *magnalia Dei* in history. Here Christians are true heirs of Judaism, for the whole Old Testament recounts the history of God's action. The Gospels continue this narrative with their account of the eternal Word made flesh and acting within history.

An excellent example is Psalm 78, a long piece of narrative that is hardly "sweet and comforting" and that can be rather daunting when it turns up at a weekday Matins. But to place it in its original context brings it to life. Picture a group of children sitting around their teacher, reciting after him the history of their people:

> Hear my teaching, O my people; incline your ears to the words of my mouth. I will open my mouth in a parable; I will declare the mysteries of ancient times. That which we have heard and known, and what our forefathers have told us, we will not hide from their

children. We will recount to generations to come the praiseworthy deeds and the power of the Lord, and the wonderful works he has done.[5]

This is oral history at its best, a type of oral history that has existed in many cultures and that is the foundation of all of our modern written records. (The Finnish national epic the *Kalevala* opens with very similar words.) The Psalm then goes on to tell the story of the Exodus, of the taking of the Promised Land, and of the rise of David as king. It recounts both the people's repeated betrayals and God's continued faithfulness. Further, it makes this recital into an act of praise, a "eucharistic" act. It not only remembers but remembers with thanksgiving, recognizes the hand of God in the history it recounts, and blesses God in all his works. This is the scriptural way to use history, to bless God for all that he has done and is doing.

So as Christians we are constantly called to "remember," and to remember in thanksgiving. We do this in several ways and on several levels. The central act of Christian worship is the Sunday Eucharist, where the community gathers to obey Jesus' command, "Do this in remembrance of me": do this, that is, remembering all that Jesus is and does and has done, and the whole of salvation history. Here we not only tell the Story; we act it. This *anamnesis*, this remembering, takes us out of ordinary time into sacred time and makes our lives a reliving of our history. Our culture is in danger of forgetting how to do this. When we as Christians renew our memory and our story, we are enriching and deepening our common life and reconnecting to our heritage.

Liturgical remembering is not purely verbal, purely a matter of reading and hearing the Scriptures. It also uses actions and material objects, involving the whole of our humanity. It may well be that the Middle Ages sometimes lost the proper balance, neglecting the preaching of the Word and turning the Mass into something not far from a magical rite. But some of the Reformation traditions have been unbalanced in the opposite direction, denying all external forms *except* the preaching of the Word. The modern "Liturgical

5. Psalm 78:1-4; *The Book of Common Prayer,* pp. 694-95.

Movement" has sought to restore this balance so that Christian worship proclaims the Word of God in both speech and action, the whole service fully intelligible to the people. Underlying this balance is the principle of *sacrament*, defined (in the old Anglican formula) as "an outward and visible sign of an inward and spiritual grace." Man is both body and spirit, and the Word is expressed to him both in tangible things — the water of Baptism, the bread and wine of the Eucharist — and in written or spoken words.

The weekly Eucharist is not the only anamnesis we have. The Divine Office — Morning and Evening Prayer, the Liturgy of the Hours — especially when it is recited daily as it is in a monastic community, retells the scriptural story. The Psalms summarize the story, reflect on it, and turn it into praise. The continuous reading of the rest of Scripture keeps the worshiping community constantly in its living stream. The Church Year is designed to spread out this telling so that we can consider one aspect at a time, beginning and ending with Advent and always returning to the central events at Holy Week and Easter. This is why the Easter Vigil is traditionally the preferred time for Holy Baptism. Baptism brings the new Christian into the very heart of the Christian story in the commemoration of the death and resurrection of Christ.

We can and should do the same thing in another way in our personal reading of the Scriptures. This is one meaning of "meditation": reading the Bible prayerfully and entering into its story as our own. I vividly recall reading the account of the Exodus for the first time in my early teens and recognizing it as somehow "my" story in a simple yet puzzling way. Some years later I discovered with surprise that many other Christians have also identified with these events. The story of all is the story of each. Furthermore, the Christian story does not end neatly, bang, at the close of the New Testament canon. The book of Acts closes in the middle of an episode, leaving Paul under house arrest in Rome; the story merges seamlessly into "Church History." This means further that we can broaden our "remembering," extend and deepen our understanding of our personal and corporate Story, by much of the other reading that we do. History and the lives of our fellow Christians in any and all centuries become our own story, for we are all contemporaries in

Christ's "sacred time." Sometimes today one hears the idea that the Gospel "makes all things new" in the sense that the past should be forgotten and only the present moment matters. The approach to memory taken here is much broader than that, maintaining that "ongoing revelation" builds on and presupposes all that has gone before, always enlarging our range of vision and our understanding but never losing what has already been.

Doubtless your friend Meg will not absorb all of these ideas at once. But when she has shared in the experience of Christian worship, and if she has learned something of its background, she should be able to glimpse something of the scope of the Christian "Story." She is probably asking more searching questions by now. The essays that follow address in more depth various aspects of the recalling and retelling of the Story. Some deal with liturgy and Scripture and their complex interrelationships. Others address the Christian life, especially as it is lived in community, and various approaches to prayer and to reading. A common thread is the Benedictine, monastic approach to the interweaving of worship and life in our own chapter of the one Story.

2 The Bible as the Ground of Our Story

Reading the Bible

Both Christians and Jews have always looked to the Bible as a primary ground of their faith, as God's revelation to the covenant community, as "inspired" in a sense that other literatures and ways of knowing are not. Thus, among a thinking Christian's first questions needs to be just how he is to read, study, and interpret Holy Scripture, and what place the Bible has in his faith, prayer, and daily life. For our present purpose, we will first consider Scripture in itself and then turn to its proclamation in the liturgy.

The Bible is, however, not a simple, clear-cut document, all of one piece and all of the same kind. It is an entire library, dating from many different times and containing many types of literature: historical narratives, straightforward commandments and legislation, poetry, writings that tell a story but do not seem to be "history" in the modern sense, and a number of other things as well. The informed reader or student of the Bible needs to recognize these various types of writing and to read and interpret each one appropriately.

The task of interpreting the writings of Scripture and of deciding how to apply them has always raised questions. Even today we hear highly diverse voices, ranging from an entrenched literalism to a liberalism that claims to rewrite Scripture according to its own canons. One claim, for example, is that Jesus *cannot* possibly have said some of the things attributed to him, and therefore he didn't: those sayings can simply be edited out of the Gospels. This piece of circular reasoning seems to allow the reader to decide what the Bible says. That would leave no reason for reading the Bible at all.

Different types of literature need to be read and interpreted differently. A Christian who accepts the Bible as the Word of God will come to it in faith, expecting to find God's truth. But he will still need to ask how that truth is being conveyed in each particular context. A straightforward literal reading soon runs into all kinds of difficulties, especially in the Old Testament. These problems are not a modern discovery: the earliest Christian writers recognized them clearly and found ways to deal with them. Saint Paul, presumably following rabbinic precedents, found allegory in the story of Abraham: Hagar and Sarah are two covenants, the one of slavery, the other of freedom: "which things are an allegory" (Gal. 4:24, KJV). Medieval writers, following a suggestion of Origen in the third century, were fond of interpreting Scripture on four levels at once:

— The *letter* shows us what God and our fathers did;
— The *allegory* shows us where our faith is hid;
— The *moral* meaning gives us rules of daily life,
— The *anagogy* shows us where we end our strife.[1]

Thus, "Jerusalem" may refer literally to the city in the Near East, allegorically to the Church, morally (or tropologically) to the human soul, or anagogically to the heavenly city. Gregory of Nyssa, in his fourth-century *Life of Moses*, develops at length and with great insight the parallels between Moses' journey with the people of Israel out of Egypt, across the Red Sea, and through the desert and the pil-

---

1. Quoted by A. Berkeley Mickelsen in *Interpreting the Bible* (Grand Rapids: Wm. B. Eerdmans, 1963), p. 35.

grimage of the soul from sin to God.[2] When viewed beside this long and rich tradition of multilayered interpretation, the arguments sometimes heard today about where Cain found a wife or what kind of fish swallowed Jonah can seem rather shallow.

More recently, research in ancient texts and languages and the spread of a "scientific" (perhaps "materialistic" would be more accurate) worldview have complicated the issues even further. Yet succeeding generations of Christians have continued to find that the Bible is more than large enough to embrace human learning, provided that we come with "faith seeking understanding" rather than with an attitude of setting ourselves in judgment above the text. The complications may require work, but in the end the Word still shines through, only the richer for the new dimensions that have been found.

For example, a literalist view would hold — and for many centuries most readers of the Bible assumed — that Eden was a concrete geographical place, Adam and Eve were identifiable individuals at a specific date in the relatively recent past, and all the events of the early chapters of Genesis are reported as in a newspaper account. Many people today, including many orthodox Christians, will broaden their reading of these chapters and see them as a profoundly true "myth." Without insisting on a literal or journalistic reading, they will see the truths that God created the whole world and gave man moral freedom, and that man abused that freedom, and they will realize that these truths apply to Adam — that is, to Everyman.

Questions raised by the Enlightenment and Darwin have caused difficulties for people trying to understand the revelation of God while living in the mental climate of a scientific, pragmatic, and skeptical culture. Chief among these are issues raised by biblical criticism, scientific developments (especially the theory of evolution), and the growth of anthropology and intercultural studies.

The simplistic approach for many people, not only the well ed-

2. Selections from this text are available in *From Glory to Glory*, selected by Jean Daniélou, S.J., trans. and ed. by Herbert Musurillo, S.J. (New York: Charles Scribner's Sons, 1961).

ucated, has been to say, "Modern science proves that Christianity is a lot of superstitious nonsense. The Bible is simply the folk history of a primitive people. We can't believe all that any more." It is interesting, however, that some of the best-educated scientific thinkers themselves are believing and practicing Christians. The contradictions are at the superficial, popular level, not at the level of developed doctrine.

The essays that follow in this chapter address the specific areas of biblical criticism, evolutionary theory, and comparative mythology. Their purpose is to show how a believing Christian can work with modern knowledge, and how a scientifically educated modern can embrace the Christian faith with mind as well as heart.

Honeycombs and Bible Critics

One fine spring morning a good many years ago, I sat in my college dorm reading Morning Prayer. The Eastertide lesson was from Luke 24: "'Have ye here any meat?' And they gave him a piece of a broiled fish, and of an honeycomb. And he took it, and did eat before them." I was fairly familiar with the King James Version in those days, and I got to thinking about that honeycomb. On the far side of the Resurrection there is room for things like honeycombs, and the heavenly banquet, and the manna, and all that. But on this particular day I was reading the lesson in Greek. "And they gave him a piece of broiled fish." Period, or at least colon. End of clause. No honeycomb. Also, and emphatically, end of meditation, at least of *that* meditation.

What happened to that honeycomb? Fortunately, I had been taught enough about textual criticism to find out. The honeycomb is in the King James because it was in the Vulgate and in the Greek manuscripts consulted by the KJV translators. But a good many more ancient manuscripts have become available since the sixteenth century, and my notes told me that Codex Bezae in particular did not include the honeycomb. Now this codex is full of additions, interpolations, and comments — any scrap of possible text the copyist could find — so anything it does *not* contain is almost certainly not original. So much is this an "assured conclusion of modern scholarship" that the RSV, the Jerusalem Bible, and the New English Bible do not contain the honeycomb either. It does survive, I note now, in one of the antiphons in our monastic Office for Paschaltide.

So what? What does textual criticism — and, along with it, other more ambitious forms of scientific biblical and historical research — have to do with the life of Christian prayer and discipleship? A number of approaches to this question have been suggested. One extreme is to consider all these tools as inventions of the devil to destroy our faith: that honeycomb is part of my prayer, and you aren't going to take it away from me. The opposite pole makes scholarship an absolute: if the "authorities," or my readings of the particular authorities I choose to consult, eliminate the honeycomb — or the resurrection or the divinity of Christ — then those things must go. A third approach is to keep prayer and scholarship in separate, watertight compartments: I do all the radical scholarship I please at my desk and go right on with the honeycomb in my meditation, and I never even notice any contradiction.

None of these options seems very satisfactory. Can we try "none," or perhaps "all," of the above? I think we can. The result may be a little less tidy than any of these simplistic solutions, but it does seem to provide an appropriate balance of faith and reason. The argument goes something like this.

Christians start with faith. In fact, *any* reasoned argument starts with presuppositions of some kind, even if only that reasoned argument is possible. The danger lies in arguments that conceal their presuppositions and claim to prove *everything* from scratch. It can't be done. But the place we begin is with our faith *in God*, in the living God and in Jesus Christ his Son, our Lord, not first with intellectual belief in any doctrine or formula.

Then our faith "seeks understanding," in Saint Anselm's phrase. We are to love and serve God with our minds as well as our hearts. God has given us Holy Scripture, and generations of learned theologians, and the research tools of modern scholarship. If we want to understand as much as we can of God's revelation, we need to use all these things. We need to know what the best texts of Scripture are, what wise writers of other ages have said about them, and what their context and background and linguistic history have to teach us. Not every one of us needs to (or could!) master all these disciplines, but they all have their place in the Church's teaching. And we must do our scholarship honestly. It is dishonest to insist on that honeycomb no matter what the texts say. It is dishonest to decide on theological grounds, whether traditional or radically modern, what the text "ought" to say and edit accordingly. A phrase like "the consensus of modern scholarship" is easily abused and may sometimes mean only "my opinion" or "my pastor's opinion."

But this scholarship, this academic Bible study, remains linked with and becomes part of our prayer. If I found material for prayer in that honeycomb, fine; but if study tells me the honeycomb doesn't belong, then I must also pray the text without it and see what its absence has to teach me. If we believe that God has truly revealed himself in the incarnate Word and in the word of Scripture, we have nothing to fear from this approach. And since we know that the words of Scripture have been transmitted through the minds, languages, and hands of men, we will not be surprised to find oddities and apparent inconsistencies. Our study may disabuse us of some simplistic answers and ingrained prejudices, but it cannot separate us from God if we hold on to faith and humility and common sense.

Two recent books illustrate these principles nicely: Avery Brooke's *Finding God in the World*[3] and John Hick's *The Metaphor of God Incarnate*.[4] Both titles would seem to suggest a similar "theology of immanence," but the two move in opposite directions and are different to the point of being almost entirely opposed. *Finding God in the World* narrates the author's journey beginning with her discovery of (by?) God, and continuing in faith to a remarkable depth of theology and spirituality. *The Metaphor of God Incarnate*, on the other hand, dismisses the traditional concept of "incarnation" as meaningless and replaces it with an academic idea of "metaphor" that

3. Avery Brooke, *Finding God in the World: Reflections on a Spiritual Journey* (Cambridge, Mass.: Cowley Publications, 1994).

4. John Hick, *The Metaphor of God Incarnate: Christology in a Pluralistic Age* (Louisville: Westminster/John Knox Press, 1993).

leaves little room for either theology or faith. The fullness of Scripture and of Christian faith has much more to offer than this.

All Ye Brontosauruses, Bless Ye the Lord

Some young friends of ours have a Noah's ark with a parade of delightful beasts, including a pair of dinosaurs (*Allosaurus*, I think). Another friend is teaching science in a "Christian" school, where apparently she is expected to lead bright, intellectually curious twelve-year-olds through the Museum of Natural History and then tell them that species are fixed and can never evolve because the Bible says so. A prominent and popular science writer claims, on the other hand, that evolution is so random and chaotic that it proves there can be no design in the universe, and therefore no Designer. What's going on here?

I have some training in science, history, and Christian theology, and I have long found these disciplines complementary and mutually enriching, not conflicting. I did feel a bit strange when my first assignment as a timid novice almost forty years ago was teaching high-school biology, but that was primarily because of a different cultural incongruity: the atmosphere of the Community's novitiate in those days was neither academic nor "modern." But when the publishers sent us the anti-evolution edition of the textbook, we sent it back with a firm note of protest. I thought the whole science-versus-religion war, or at least the part of it concerned with evolutionary theory, had been retired to a well-deserved obscurity after the Scopes "monkey trial" seventy years ago. Judging by some of what is being said today, it seems I was wrong.

"Do you believe in God, or do you believe in evolution?" Just how is anyone supposed to answer a question like that? But, since it is still being asked seriously, let me try to clarify several points.

How is the term "evolution" being used? The first question is whether we are talking about biology or metaphysics. Properly, "evolution" is a shorthand summary of a scientific hypothesis describing certain observed facts about the natural world. Popularly, it sometimes slides into "Evolution," an almost-personified blind

Force that somehow rules nature — a false god. Only when the second sense is present do we need to choose between God and a meaningless blind Force.

What does it mean to "believe"? This word also has several meanings, and confusing them causes another of the difficulties here. I *believe* in God, and I believe that God made (and makes) the world and everything in it. I believe that God has revealed (and reveals) himself in history, in the Bible, and uniquely in the Incarnate Christ. This kind of belief is part of faith; it involves personal relationship and commitment. I do not in this sense "believe" that Moses wrote the Pentateuch in its present form (or that he didn't, for that matter), or that the serpent spoke to Eve in letter-perfect Hebrew, or that the earth is either round or flat. These are questions for a different kind of cognition, not for "belief."

A scientific theory is something else altogether. It begins life as a hypothesis, an educated guess, about a possible explanation for some natural phenomenon. If, after considerable study, it seems to fit quite a wide range of evidence, make it intelligible, and predict further phenomena, it graduates to being a "theory." But it remains a negotiable thing, always subject to further revision and addition as new evidence is found. It is not so much "true" or "false" as it is more or less *useful*. Old theories never die (well, hardly ever); instead, they are amended so much that they become new theories. So the "theory of evolution" is not so much something to *believe* as it is a model or diagram or method for understanding a lot of biology, and one that most people trained in biology today find generally a useful one.[5]

Where then does the Bible fit into these categories? Does one *believe* it or treat it as a source of factual information? Both. I believe the Bible, or rather believe in the God whom it reveals; it conveys God's revelation of himself. This revelation is primarily of *God*, not primarily of details of scientific or historical facts. We go to the Bible primarily with questions that science cannot answer, ques-

5. The principal source for this paragraph, and for much of this section, is Eric Mascall's *Christian Theology and Natural Science* (London: Longmans, Green & Co., 1956).

tions like where the world came from and why, and how we are supposed to behave in it. I suppose God could have given us a simple, unambiguous, itemized set of revelations about himself if he had wanted to, but it seems he has not done so. We have four Gospels, not one, and anyone who has tried harmonizing them knows that they don't match smoothly and easily. I don't see where the Bible says anything about the immutability of species one way or the other (though the historical information in the Bible can often be shown to be much more trustworthy than the skeptics want to concede). So the Bible is the Word of God and tells us what we need to know and believe for our souls' health, but scientific studies such as archaeology, textual criticism, and linguistic research are legitimate and helpful in understanding the whole of God's work.

The best book that I know in this area is *Christian Theology and Natural Science,* the Bampton Lectures for 1956 by English theologian Eric Mascall. Today the science needs updating rather than correcting, and the theology is both sound and quite readable for anyone even moderately versed in its technical language. Since these were originally lectures, and since the author was gifted with a sense of humor, they are even witty.

Back to those dinosaurs trying to board Noah's ark. We all know, don't we, that the unicorns missed the ark because they were too proud to get on, and the dinosaurs missed it because they were too big or too stupid or both, and that's why there are no unicorns or dinosaurs today. That's flippant. We also all know that the dinosaurs had been gone for 65 million years before Noah was born. That's irrelevant. The story of the ark tells us, among other things, that God has made a covenant with all living things, and that we humans have a role of stewardship in this covenant. That message certainly is appropriate today! A study of dinosaurs (or viruses or the moons of Jupiter) tells us that God's creation is more complicated, and more wonderful, than we knew. That message is appropriate too. And Christians with any bent for science and natural history can do a good deal to glorify God and to proclaim his Word, *both* by reading their Bibles carefully *and* by doing their science as honestly and thoroughly as they can.

Glorify the Lord, *all* you works of the Lord.

Myth and Mystery

The word "myth" has at least two meanings. The popular meaning is "a pretty story that isn't true." The dictionary meaning (simplified) is "a story that is told to explain something else, often a religious belief or practice, or a very deep truth." A contemporary writer has defined it as "a symbolic story intended to express truth, and a truth perhaps best apprehended and understood through story."[6] A myth points to a mystery. A myth is something like a parable, because the point of it is in the meaning of the story and does not depend on whether the story is newspaper-reporter "true" or documented "history." Sometimes it is "true" in that sense, sometimes not, and sometimes we just don't know. The important "truth" of the myth is in another dimension.

All cultures have myths, and very similar myths are found in widely different cultures. Stories of the creation of man, of a flood, of a god who dies and rises — these are found in many cultures. Christian writers as early as Justin Martyr in the second century realized this and dealt with it by giving a variety of explanations ranging from "falsehoods created by the Devil" to "foreshadowings inspired by the Holy Spirit." At the beginning of the twentieth century, the growth of comparative anthropology and comparative literature made Christians, already disturbed by other developments, uncomfortably aware of all these parallels. The publication of *The Golden Bough* by Sir James George Frazer over the years 1890-1915 and its influence on T. S. Eliot in *The Waste Land* (1922) led many people to conclude that Christianity is just another "myth" in the bad sense and can be ignored.

The experience of C. S. Lewis with regard to the whole question of "myth" is typical of many people of his own generation and of others. As an adolescent he discovered the pagan myths, particularly in his case the Norse ones, and found them profoundly attractive

---

6. Stratford Caldecott, "Speaking the Truths Only the Imagination May Grasp: Myth and 'Real Life,'" *Touchstone* 11:5 (Sept./Oct. 1998): 44. This essay is also included in *The Pilgrim's Guide: C. S. Lewis and the Art of Witness,* ed. David Mills (Grand Rapids: Wm. B. Eerdmans, 1998), pp. 86-97. The entire essay, which appeared after this chapter was essentially complete, expresses very eloquently much the same position on "myth" as that adopted here but uses it in a somewhat different way.

without thinking they were in any sense "true." Realizing that Christian story contains many of the same elements and not finding it attractive at all, he dismissed that too as being a man-made fiction. His (re)conversion to Christianity as an adult was closely involved with a new understanding of how myth can convey important truth. This was largely taught him by Hugo Dyson and J. R. R. Tolkien; an all-night conversation in September 1931 was pivotal. He recounted this experience at length in a letter to his friend Arthur Greeves:

> Now what Dyson and Tolkien showed me was that if I met the idea of sacrifice in a Pagan story I didn't mind it at all: again, that if I met the idea of a god sacrificing himself to himself (cf. the quotation opposite the title page of *Dymer*) I liked it very much and was mysteriously moved by it: again, that the idea of the dying and reviving god (Balder, Adonis, Bacchus) similarly moved me provided I met it anywhere *except* in the Gospels. The reason was that in Pagan stories I was prepared to feel the myth as profound and suggestive of meanings beyond my grasp even tho' I could not say in cold prose "what it meant." Now the story of Christ is simply a true myth: a myth working on us in the same way as the others, but with this tremendous difference that *it really happened:* and one must be content to accept it in the same way, remembering that it is God's myth where the other are men's myths: i.e. the Pagan stories are God expressing Himself through the minds of poets, using such images as He found there, while Christianity is God expressing Himself through what we call "real things." Therefore it is *true,* not in the sense of being a "description" of God (that no finite mind would take in) but in the sense of being the way in which God chooses to (or can) appear to our faculties. The "doctrines" we get *out of* the true myth are of course *less* true: they are translations into our *concepts* and *ideas* of that which God has already expressed in a language more adequate, namely the actual incarnation, crucifixion, and resurrection.[7]

7. Letter from C. S. Lewis to Arthur Greeves, quoted in *C. S. Lewis: A Biography,* by Roger Lancelyn Green and Walter Hooper (New York and London: Harcourt Brace Jovanovich, 1974), pp. 117-18.

Lewis's resolution, and a useful one, is to say that yes, there is a "Christian myth": the difference is that *the Christian myth is a myth that really happened.* Jesus fulfilled all the archetypes of the "dying god," and he also was a real person: he lived, he died "under Pontius Pilate," and he rose again. This is central to Christian faith. If he didn't rise, and if that tomb wasn't empty on that Sunday morning, there would be no Christians today. The Gospel was first preached by those frightened disciples who had run away to hide, then met their risen Lord and promptly went out as changed men, boldly to proclaim him as Lord and God.

Jesus is as real to the journalist or the historian as Julius Caesar or Socrates. That is essential. Saying that doesn't have to mean that all the "stories" in the Bible are "history" in the same sense. Genesis is part of the "teaching" section of the Old Testament, not of the "historical" books. We don't have to know whether a man named Adam and a woman named Eve had an argument with a snake (where? when? in Hebrew?) to see the point of the story: at some time, a single human being (or rather, two) made the first moral choice, and made it wrong. On the other hand, we do know that a real girl named Mary had a conversation with an angel (however we are supposed to understand that). This did happen. She made a moral choice too, and she made it right. Finding the boundaries between history and myth in the Bible, with all the intermediate grades of part-history and idealized history and myth with a kernel of history, is a legitimate task for the scholar. Discerning the Word of God in any of these expressions is the role of faith, for each in its own way conveys the eternal Truth in human language. Caldecott expresses this idea especially well, calling it the principle of "Maximum Possible Meaning": "Wherever the text of the Bible does not appear to contradict itself, or is not contradicted by human reason or by certain knowledge from some other sources, tradition encourages us to assume that it is *literally* as well as symbolically true — that is, true to the surface as well as to the inner life of the world."[8]

8. Caldecott, "Speaking the Truths Only the Imagination May Grasp," p. 45.

3 The Story in the Liturgy

The Bible is central to Christian faith and is the charter of the Christian community. The primary setting for the Bible is the liturgy, the work of the *laos,* the people of God. God's covenant, in the biblical tradition, is primarily with the *people* rather than with individuals. The early Church understood very well the unity of these three themes: Bible, covenant people, and liturgy. It was the late Middle Ages and the Enlightenment that lost sight of the unity and developed both an untraditional individualism and the anomalous conflict between a "Catholic," clericalized, mechanical liturgy and a "Protestant," anti-clerical, anti-liturgical biblicism. The great achievement of the so-called Liturgical Movement of the twentieth century, in the Roman Catholic and other churches, has been the recovery of the corporate nature of liturgy and its foundation in the Bible.[1] The natural setting for the reading of Scripture is the community gathered for worship, with the Word read and relived liturgically for all to share.[2] The liturgy is first and foremost simply the dramatic proclamation of the Scriptures. Of course, the Psalms are

---

1. An excellent Anglican introduction to this movement, and one that was itself important in introducing the movement into England, is A. G. Hebert's *Liturgy and Society* (London: Faber & Faber, 1935).

2. A classic example of this is Ezra's reading of the Law to the people in Nehemiah 8–13. See also Colossians 4:16 and Revelation 1:3.

pre-eminently the "prayer book" of the Bible; the corporate recitation of the Psalms is and always has been the mainstay of Christian corporate prayer, especially in the monastic tradition.

Central to the biblical way of doing things is the remembering of God's mighty deeds by retelling the story, in some sense re-enacting it, and so entering into its historic reality in a "sacred time" that is outside ordinary time. The Jewish Passover celebration is an excellent example of this: "What mean ye by this service?" The Christian Church has inherited this practice, especially in the more liturgical traditions, and her liturgy is the reliving and the *anamnesis*, the memory, of God's saving deeds in history. This takes place in several ways and on several levels. Every celebration of the Eucharist recapitulates the entire Christian story; on a larger scale, the observance of the Church Year, centered in the Easter Vigil, spells it out in detail. As Hebert observes:

> Liturgical forms, like drama, are composed in order to be enacted; and again, they differ from drama, in that there is no audience, and all those present share in the action; if anyone is present merely as an onlooker, he misses all the meaning that matters.[3]

Liturgy is a form of drama; in fact, modern secular drama as we know it originated in liturgy, both Greek and Christian. As drama it has a cast, the people of God assembled for worship, with special roles and functions assigned to many of the participants. In our egalitarian time it is worth noting that these assignments are not random, not ordinarily self-chosen, and not all alike. There is a definite hierarchy here, and a "leader" who is not simply one among others, and not necessarily chosen for his natural gifts or his "worth," but an appointed head who is in some sense a representative and an icon of God himself as Father, Shepherd, and Ruler of his people. This hierarchical ordering is part of the way the Bible presents community. It does not in any way contradict the idea that all are of equal worth in the sight of God. The drama has a setting, a sacred space, and an ordered structure that employs carefully

3. Hebert, *Liturgy and Society*, p. 246.

planned movements and visual effects to express its meaning. A liturgical procession is not a mere frill, but a proclamation and a representation of the people of God on pilgrimage, "with the Cross of Jesus going on before," as a familiar hymn says. But most of all the drama tells a Story, the same story we have discussed already in more detail. But it is the same Story from beginning to end — God's loving action, man's refusal of that action and of God's love, and God's new action making new life possible.

The Easter Liturgy

Easter is of course the center and heart of Christian liturgical observance. Probably the greatest single achievement of the Liturgical Movement of this century has been the restoration and enhancement of the traditional Paschal liturgy, encompassing the depths and heights of the drama of Redemption. The 1928 Episcopal Prayer Book made no provision either for a special Good Friday liturgy or for an Easter Vigil. The usual Good Friday service a generation or two ago was the Three-Hour preaching service. Where Easter Even was observed at all, the unofficial forms in use provided only for lighting the Paschal candle and singing the *Exsultet*. "Easter Service" meant a Sunday like other Sundays except for extra music, special hymns, and lots of flowers.

Many of us older ones can remember vividly how puzzling and yet how exciting an old-style Orthodox vigil was (hours of incomprehensible Slavonic chanting, and marching around a church in the inner city in the middle of the night), as were the newly restored full Western services when we first met them as adults. For American Anglicans, this liturgy is now found in the material provided for Maundy Thursday, Good Friday, and the Easter Vigil in the 1979 Book of Common Prayer. These really form a single whole, beginning with the footwashing of the Maundy Thursday evening Eucharist. We not only "remember" Jesus' actions at the Last Supper; we reenact them as he told us to do. The service is usually followed by an all-night, or part-night, vigil before the reserved Sacrament, in memory of Gethsemane. The Good Friday service is not simply a preaching service but a liturgical reading of Scripture, especially the solemn reading of the Saint John Passion with the entire congregation participating. It is we ourselves who cry with the crowd, "Crucify him!" The starkness of the day is emphasized by the fact that there is no celebration of the Eucharist, only the readings, and perhaps Holy Communion from the Sacrament reserved for the Thursday night watch, an accepting of and sharing in the Lord's self-offering. This starkness, and the silent, empty waiting of Holy Saturday, lead up to the climax of the Easter Vigil.

The service begins outside the church and in the dark, usually on Saturday evening but ideally before dawn on Sunday: the darkness of the world that does not know the Resurrection. Here in the dark the celebrant kindles a new fire and lights the Paschal candle. The symbol of light in darkness, and of light as abiding presence, is universal and fundamental, much older than Christianity. Then the congregation moves in procession into the church, and the deacon sings the *Exsultet*. This seventh-century text proclaims not the historical narrative of Jesus' resurrection and the empty tomb but the theological meaning of God's triumph over darkness and death both in the Passover and in the Resurrection:

> This is the night, when you brought our fathers, the children of Israel, out of bondage in Egypt, and led them through the Red Sea on dry land. This is the night, when all who believe in Christ are delivered from the gloom of sin, and are restored to grace and holiness of life. This is the night, when Christ broke the bonds of death and hell, and rose victorious from the grave.[4]

All of salvation history becomes present. "Darkness has been vanquished by our mighty King" in all these ways, all symbolized by the new light of the Paschal candle and the people's small candles, blazing in the still-darkened church. This symbolism of the New Fire speaks, as it is meant to do, at a much deeper level than the verbal. Then the church lights are turned on, and the service continues

---

4. The *Exsultet*, from *The Book of Common Prayer* (New York: Oxford University Press, 1979), p. 287.

with "the record of God's saving deeds in history." The Scriptures come alive. These are no longer remote historical accounts or just "Bible readings." We are *there*, at the Red Sea, in the Ark, even watching Creation happen. That is the point of liturgy, and that is why liturgy is a tremendous tool of evangelism.

The rubrics provide nine Old Testament lessons for this service, requiring that at least two be used, one of them the Crossing of the Red Sea from Exodus. Even with a small congregation, however, it is perfectly possible to use all nine, each read by a different member of the congregation and each followed by a sung Psalm or canticle and a collect, and so to experience the whole scope of salvation history.

But what is the point of all these readings? Isn't Easter about Jesus rising from the dead? Why not read that Gospel account and have done with it?

The basic structure of this Vigil is grounded in a definite theology of revelation. This, which can probably fairly be called the classical Christian view, is that God's revelation is in and through history, not in a set of abstractions, and it is a single revelation throughout that history. The living God speaks and acts in the history of Israel as recorded in the Old Testament Scriptures, and this revelation is fulfilled but not abrogated in Christ. So the Vigil prepares for the celebration of the Resurrection by recounting the whole history that leads up to it. We are doing *anamnesis* here, recollection, re-presentation, "making memorial" in a very real way, just as we do in the Eucharist.

The typological approach, whereby one event foreshadows or fulfills another, and God's truth is revealed on several different levels at once, is a traditional and very fruitful way of reading the Scriptures. Hence, "Let us hear the record of God's saving deeds in history, how he saved his people in ages past." This history is *our* history. The Resurrection as a concrete, factual event is the climax of this history, not a single (and for some people even problematic) event to be considered in isolation. Each of the "types" recounted in this service in some way foreshadows or typifies it. This typological way of thinking may at first seem artificial to moderns, but it is as valid today as it was for Origen and the Gregories and all the Fathers, and for that matter for the New Testament writers.

Thus the first four of these readings recount the principal, archetypal acts of God in the history of Israel. In each case the following Psalm and collect call attention to our own place in these acts. First we hear the account of Creation from Genesis 1–2, the whole story. (The first reader needs plenty of breath.) The point here is not whether these are twenty-four-hour days, or whether Adam is an individual or a people, but the vital truths that God by his Word made the world as we know it, and made us, and saw that it was "very good," and that the first man betrayed the trust given to him. Psalm 33 picks up the theme: "By the Word of the Lord were the heavens made." And the collect carries the thought beyond the first creation in Adam to the new creation in Christ: "O God, who wonderfully created and yet more wonderfully restored the dignity of human nature. . . ."

The second reading is the story of the Flood (Genesis 7–9). The popularity of Noah's ark cartoons and charming ark toys should not be allowed to obscure the main point. Men sinned against God, and God resolved to destroy the world he had made because of its sin. But he promised to save a few, a chosen remnant, if they would obey him by building an ark at his direction. Then God destroyed the world by flood, and the remnant were saved through the water. This story is a type of salvation through water, through baptism and entry into the Church. The author of 1 Peter makes this explicit: "God's patience waited in the days of Noah, during the building of the ark, in which a few, that is, eight persons, were saved through water. Baptism, which corresponds to this, now saves you . . . through the resurrection of Jesus Christ" (3:20-21). The collect expresses the appropriate response: we who have received the covenant are to offer to God the sacrifice of thanksgiving.

The third lesson, Abraham's sacrifice of Isaac in Genesis 22, is a key type of Christ as well as a key theme of the Old Covenant. Jews and Muslims also consider this passage a central one. To some modern people the whole issue of sacrifice, of a God who can ask for sacrifice, is a difficult one, and this narrative is an embarrassment. Yet sacrifice is on a profound level a fundamental theme of Scripture, and also a nearly universal archetype. In the Paschal context, it appears in the death of the firstborn, which is given as the basis for

God's claim upon all firstborn sons and therefore upon all people. In Jesus' own life, it appears in his Presentation in the temple as an infant and in his willing obedience to the Father in his Passion. Jesus himself must have meditated deeply on this story of Abraham and Isaac, and found in it his own mission as the Son of man. Isaac here is surely a figure of the Christ, of the Son who goes freely and willingly to offer his life as a sacrifice at the word of the Father. Isaac carrying the wood foreshadows Jesus carrying the cross. The ram appears in the bush, and Isaac is spared. No ram, no angel comes to save Jesus from death; but the power of the Father brings him back, trampling down death by death. If we are biblical Christians, we cannot avoid the depths of this challenge and this demand.

The fourth lesson, which is so important that it is required to be read even in a shortened Vigil, recounts the crossing of the Red Sea after the Passover (Exodus 14). The Passover feast, the saving of God's people when the angel of death "passed over" the houses marked with blood, is of course the central feast for Jews. Christ's death and resurrection fulfilled this ancient type in his "passing over" from death to life through the offering of his own blood. The whole Easter liturgy is full of Passover language, especially in the glorious *Exsultet* and in so many of the hymns: "God hath brought his Israel into joy from sadness; loosed from Pharaoh's bitter yoke Jacob's sons and daughters, led them with unmoistened foot through the Red Sea waters."[5] But at this point in the Vigil, the fulfillment is not made explicit. We remain with Moses and the people of Israel on the far side of the Red Sea, and sing with Moses, "I will sing to the Lord, for he has triumphed gloriously."

The remaining five lessons move from history to prophecy. They point to the full and final triumph of God, which we see begun and foreshadowed in the deliverances already recounted, which finds its climax in the Resurrection, and which will be completed in the last time. Two readings from Isaiah (from chapter 4 and chapter 55) foretell the glory of God and the offer of salvation: "Ho, everyone who

5. *The Hymnal 1982* (New York: The Church Hymnal Corporation, 1982), no. 199.

thirsts, come to the waters." Ezekiel prophesies the return from the Exile: "I will take you from the nations . . . and bring you into your own land" (chapter 36). The great vision of the Valley of the Dry Bones (chapter 37) foreshadows both the resurrection of Christ and the final restoration; a good reader can make it very impressive indeed. The last reading, from Zephaniah 3, is a summary and a reassurance: "The King of Israel, the Lord, is in your midst; you shall fear evil no more."

In all these readings we are still in the Old Covenant, identifying ourselves with the people of Israel. After the readings, baptism is administered, and the whole congregation renew their baptismal vows. This is the primary and most traditional time for baptisms. By this action today's congregation, today's Christians, become an integral part of the story they are recalling. Then bells are rung, and the "Great Alleluia" is sung for the first time. Finally, in the readings of the Eucharist proper, at the end of the Vigil, we hear the specifically Christian message. The Epistle, from Romans 6, identifies us with Christ in both death and resurrection: "If we have died with Christ, we believe that we shall also live with him." And at last in the Gospel we reach the central historical event to which this whole service, and the whole of the Old Testament, points. It is Matthew's account of the Resurrection (chapter 28), or rather of the women's encounter, first with the angel and then with the risen Jesus himself. Then, and only then, the service comes to its climax with the Easter Eucharist.

The Liturgy of the Eucharist

The Easter observance, of course, happens only once a year, at great length and with great intensity. But the same fundamental *anamnesis* is focused and encapsulated in every celebration of the Christian Eucharist. This service has been the central act of Christian worship on the Lord's Day from the very beginning, from the "breaking of bread" in the book of Acts (chapter 2, chapter 20) to the present day. The setting and context have varied enormously, from house church to great cathedral to prison camp, from a small country congregation to the coronation of a king to the funeral of a beloved brother. Even today, the style may vary from stately ceremony to folk gathering to the quiet, almost private "said" service. But the essential structure can always be discerned.

The service of the Eucharist, the Holy Communion, the Lord's Supper, or the Mass, as it is observed today in the Episcopal and other "liturgical" churches, falls into two parts. These were originally separate services for different congregations, but they were joined in perhaps the fourth century.[6]

The first, the Liturgy of the Word, was simply adapted from the usage of the synagogues so familiar to the first Christians, and was open both to professing Christians and to catechumens and inquirers. Today it consists of readings from Scripture, usually either two or three, one of them always from one of the Gospels. Psalms or hymns or other responses are often used before, between, and after these. Next, the presiding officer (the bishop; more about him presently) speaks to expound and explain the readings. Then, usually, the Nicene Creed is said or sung as a proclamation of faith and a summary of the teaching just heard. A series of prayers of intercession closes the first part of the service and forms a bridge to the second. In the early Church, during the days of persecution, the catechumens and any other unbaptized persons were firmly dismissed at the end of this service, either before or after the prayers. As this summary shows, this service is one of teaching and proclamation, one of *telling* the Story and thanking God for it. Many Christian "worship services" in both the Catholic and the Protestant traditions, as well as many ecumenical services, are very much like this.

The second part of the service, the Eucharist proper, has a much more dramatic structure and is concerned to *do* the Word, obeying the Lord's instructions at the Last Supper. So here the pattern is not the synagogue service but the Jewish fellowship meal, itself a ritual or liturgical action. Because Jesus himself invested this action with a new meaning, and because it has been developed in such a way as to incorporate the whole story of Redemption, it has

---

6. The detailed history of the Eucharist is very complex. For a thorough, if still somewhat controversial, treatment, see Dom Gregory Dix, *The Shape of the Liturgy* (Westminster, Eng.: The Dacre Press, 1943).

many levels of meaning. The Eucharistic action can be viewed in many ways, but perhaps one of the most helpful ones is to see it as a drama, a re-enactment and retelling of God's redemption of the world in Christ. No matter what the theme of the particular day or readings, the kernel is the same: man's rejection of God in the death of Christ, and Christ's restoration and redemption by his victory over death.

As a drama, the Eucharistic action has a structure, a setting, and a cast. While the service of readings could be rearranged, shortened, or lengthened without affecting its nature very much, the action has a beginning, a middle, and an end: offertory, then consecration, then communion. Communion before consecration would make no sense. Similarly, the service of readings could be held anywhere, and in principle an individual could read it all by himself. But the action requires at least an approximately suitable space and a gathered assembly. The Eucharist can be celebrated, and often has been, in a hospital room or a prison cell, but the setting of a consecrated building gives still another medium for expressing its meaning. There are special, appointed roles in this action. The celebrant is not simply one of the faithful but is appointed and ordained to serve both as their spokesman to God and as an icon of the presence of Christ at their head. That is why this is primarily the office of a bishop in the Church of God, or of a priest as his representative. Other members of the congregation, ordained or lay, may be assigned special roles as well, as assistants, servers, readers, oblation bearers, musicians, or ushers. The others, without specific tasks on a particular day, are, if one likes, the "chorus." It is an ordered body like an orchestra or the cast of a play, not simply an "audience" of faceless and interchangeable bodies, and there are no nonparticipating parts.

Saint Paul writes, "Whoever . . . eats the bread or drinks the cup of the Lord in an unworthy manner will be guilty of profaning the body and blood of the Lord. Let a man examine himself, and so eat of the bread and drink of the cup" (1 Cor. 11:27-28). Christians have always seen a close connection between the Lord's Supper and the forgiveness of sins, both because we are warned to prepare ourselves by self-examination and repentance before approaching the Sacrament, and because the sacramental grace of the Eucharist itself conveys God's forgiveness. The glory of Christ's victory and the reality of the new life in Christ stand out strongly precisely when we do not forget that we have been bought with a price and that, new men though we be, we also all sin repeatedly and need regularly to ask forgiveness. For many centuries no one would have dared to receive Holy Communion without having previously made a sacramental confession; this is one of the reasons why most people communicated so rarely in the Middle Ages. At the time of the English Reformation, the Book of Common Prayer introduced a corporate general confession and absolution within the Eucharistic service itself. For a time, so much emphasis was laid on this that it seemed as if forgiveness was the only reason for the Eucharist, and other aspects of worship were slighted. Most modern liturgical revisions have generally retained a general confession, usually at the beginning of the service or before the offertory, while also reasserting the importance of worship, proclamation, fellowship, and newness of life. Omitting confession and penitence altogether, as is sometimes done, suggests a Pollyanna sort of religion in which everything is just fine; there is no more sin or pain or sorrow in the world, no need to acknowledge responsibility, to repent, or to ask forgiveness for anything.

The Eucharistic action begins with the offertory, in which bread, wine, and often other gifts are brought to the altar and presented to God. This is sometimes misunderstood as our giving something to God so that he will give us something in return. It is not that; of ourselves we have nothing at all that we *can* offer to God. The only "offering" that will take place in this service is the *anamnesis* of Christ's own offering to the Father. All the offertory can do is to prepare the materials for this offering, to bring our gifts and so "ourselves, our souls and bodies" to be taken up into Christ's offering. The offertory often includes a procession of representatives from the congregation carrying the people's gifts and the bread and wine to be used for the Eucharist; the revival of this very ancient custom is another of the positive fruits of the Liturgical Movement.

The Eucharistic Prayer, or the Canon, or the Great Thanksgiving, the central prayer of the Eucharist, has existed and exists today in many different forms. The root of this prayer is the Jewish prayer of blessing, which praises God for his acts, his gifts, and his great glory, and in so doing consecrates the thing that is blessed. In this prayer the celebrant, speaking and acting in the name of Christ and leading the congregation, does several things. He praises and blesses God for being God (the Sanctus) and commemorates God's work in creation and in history, and especially in the Redemption in Christ. Then, obeying the command of Christ and acting as Christ's representative, he "takes" the bread, and the other offerings, "blesses, breaks, and gives." By this blessing Christ's one sacrifice is made present, and we are taken up into it. This is a "commemoration," but a special one, an *anamnesis,* because the commemoration "makes present" the original action. Another way to look at it is to say that the Eucharistic action takes today's congregation right out of time and into eternity. Their praise and offering are taken up into the one offering that Christ alone made once for all, and so made part of the only offering that can be acceptable to the Father.

Anglican theologian Dr. Eric Mascall summarizes this action as follows:

> The offering begins when the celebrant offers the bread and wine to God as Christ offered them at the Last Supper and identifies what he is doing now with what Christ did then. The Father accepts the plea that is made in the name of his Son, and in accepting what is offered he transforms it. What began by being an offering of creatures of bread and wine has been transformed into the offering of the Body and Blood of Christ; the sacrifice of the Church has become the sacrifice of Christ. . . . And when the faithful come up to the altar to receive Holy Communion, the truth is not so much that the Body and Blood of Christ are being given to them for their sanctification as that they are being drawn up into Christ for the building up of his Body; the Sacrament does not disperse Christ among the faithful, it unites the faithful in Christ. And so, in the words of St. Augustine, it is shown to the Church that in that which she offers she herself is offered. . . . Thus there is not first an offering to God of bread and wine at the offertory and then a second offering to God of the Body and Blood of Christ in the canon after the consecration. There is one offering,

an offering of bread and wine which, being transformed by the divine acceptance, *becomes* the offering of the Body and Blood; and it takes place in the canon. . . .

The essence of the Eucharist is the one great action of the Eucharistic canon, which is able to offer the Church's gifts to God solely because it consecrates them into things that are worthy to be offered. There is not first an offering and then a consecration, for not until the consecration are the gifts fit for offering. But neither, on the other hand, is there first a consecration and then an offering, for the consecration is simply the transformation by God's acceptance of the gifts that are offered to him. There is one prayer, the great Eucharistic Prayer, which simultaneously consecrates and offers in one action; which offers by consecrating and consecrates by offering and does both by giving thanks.[7]

After the celebrant breaks the consecrated bread, he gives the bread that is now the true Body of our Lord to the communicants. The anthem *Agnus Dei*, which is often sung here, and the old and still much-loved "Prayer of Humble Access" remind us again that we are unworthy sinners and ask for God's mercy. By Holy Communion we are united to Christ and his offering, and to one another, in action and in the body as well as in word and prayer. This is not the place for an extended discussion of the "Eucharistic presence." Suffice it to say that classic Christian doctrine from the earliest times has acknowledged the "Real Presence" of the risen Christ in the consecrated elements. The reductionist positions that speak only of a "memorial" or an "act of faith" owe most of their existence to the nominalist philosophy of the late Middle Ages, which simply had no mental tools for understanding a reality that is not seen or a creature that can have two natures, two meanings at the same time.[8]

When the action is completed, the service ends quickly. After a prayer of thanksgiving, the people are dismissed with a blessing to

7. Eric L. Mascall, *Corpus Christi* (London: Longmans, Green & Co., 1953), chap. 6, pp. 179-82. The entire book is the foundation for much of this section.
8. For more on this, see Dr. Mascall's *The Recovery of Unity* (London: Longmans, Green & Co., 1958).

"Go into the world" — to *be* the people of God and to continue living out the Eucharistic action in their homes, offices, and playgrounds. When the sacramental principle is rightly understood, the Eucharist is not an isolated "religious" act but a focus that draws our entire lives into Christ. Precisely because the Eucharist is holy and a Sacrament, our common meals, our work, our fellowship, and all the other parts of our lives become holy too and, so to speak, "little-s" sacraments. The Eucharist becomes an entire way of living, with its rhythm of weekly — or often, when possible, daily — worship at the altar serving as the focus of an integrated Christian life.

4 The Litany of the Law: Psalm 119

A priest friend of ours used to decline to attend the Noon Office on Sunday, saying, "Eighty verses of Psalm 119 are a bit too much of a good thing." The Community of St. Mary's more recent revision of the *Monastic Diurnal* no longer provides quite such large helpings of that Psalm, but our friend certainly had a point. This longest of the Psalms has long been a staple of monastic corporate prayer. In this community it is still recited every week, spread over several days' Little Hours. The theme of this Psalm might be summarized as "the law of the Lord is a good thing." Each of its 176 verses says this, each in a different way. Isn't this overdoing things a little? Doesn't this become "vain repetition," or belaboring the obvious, or just plain boring?

Even admitting that Hebrew poetry is based on parallelism, finding 176 ways to say the same thing is something of a tour de force. Psalm 119 is a rather artificial literary construction in another way too, which is hinted at in the 1979 Prayer Book version. The Psalm is a carefully constructed acrostic: it is is divided into twenty-two sections of eight verses each, and all the verses in each section begin with the same Hebrew letter. This is the reason for those cryptic titles "Daleth," "Qoph," and the rest, which are, incidentally, a convenient way to learn the Hebrew alphabet.

A little careful attention to these verses as they go by, however,

36

reveals a number of other avenues of thought. One is the contrast between good and evil men: some of the verses don't say "The Law is good," but rather "The good man keeps the Law, but the wicked doesn't even know it." Studying this Psalm one section at a time — preferably *not* while trying to sing it in choir! — will reveal many such subordinate themes.

Another feature is less obvious, and since finding it took a little detective work, it might be worth sharing. The Law is mentioned in every verse (except 122), but a number of different words seem to be used for it: commandments, statutes, decrees, promises. Is this just someone's thesaurus getting tired of repetition, or is there an underlying difference in meaning?

Marshaling the appropriate books, and summoning up my extremely rudimentary Hebrew and somewhat more adequate Latin, I made an interesting discovery. The translators of our present Psalter may have taken liberties elsewhere, but here they have been quite remarkably consistent and true to the original. There are indeed ten different words used for "the Law" in the Hebrew, and each is translated quite consistently by a different English word. (The Spanish edition also seems to be consistent in its use of the different terms.) Saint Jerome in the Vulgate was fairly consistent in his use of Latin equivalents, but the present English is even more so. There are very few exceptions. One word *(imrah)* is translated sometimes "word" and sometimes "promise"; but don't we do that with "word" ourselves, as in "keeping one's word"? The following table summarizes the ten words and their Latin and English equivalents.[1] Most of us know *Torah,* and *mitzvah* as in "bar mitzvah." The distinctions among "law," "decree," "judgment," and the rest bear pondering, and seem to reflect real underlying differences in meaning.

All this attention to the Law naturally brings to mind Saint Paul and his apparent attacks upon it. Could Saul the Jew continue to recite this Psalm as Paul the Christian? He writes about the *abolition* of the law of commandments and ordinances, three of our words in one phrase. Surely, however, there is no real contradiction

1. The transliterations given are from R. M. Benson's *The War Songs of the Prince of Peace* (New York: E. P. Dutton & Co., 1901), vol. 2, pp. 400-401.

here. The overarching word is the *Torah*, the purpose, revelation, and teaching of God, and one of the verbs used most frequently in relation to it seems to mean both "meditate upon" and "take delight in, relish." Psalm 119 is no more interested in petty legalism than is Saint Paul; this is the love of the Law, and the Law of love, not "justification by the works of the Law." The new covenant, the new Law, the new Torah transcends the legalism to which the old was sometimes reduced, but retains and heightens its love, its relish, for the Word. Here we have the true Law that Christ came to fulfill and the answer to all legalisms, all the little "laws" that become idols when they obscure the one Law. The Word, the *davar*, is also the *Logos*, the Word who himself became flesh and in whom we are saved.

HEBREW	LATIN (Vulgate)	ENGLISH (1979 BCP)
TORAH	lex	law
EDVOTH	testimonia	decrees
DERAKIM	viae	ways
PIQQUDIM	mandata	commandments
CHUQQIM	justificationes	statutes
MITSVOTH	mandata	commandments
MISHPATIM	judicia	judgments, decrees
IMRAH	eloquia	promises, word
DAVAR	sermo	word
EMUNAH	veritas	faithfulness

5 The Whole Armor of God

Be strong in the Lord and in the strength of his might. Put on the whole armor of God, that you may be able to stand against the wiles of the devil. For we are not contending against flesh and blood, but against the principalities, against the powers, against the world rulers of this present darkness [the rulers of the darkness of this world — KJV], against the spiritual hosts of wickedness in the heavenly places. Therefore take the whole armor of God, that you may be able to withstand in the evil day, and having done all, to stand. Stand therefore, having girded your loins with truth, and having put on the breastplate of righteousness, and having shod your feet with the equipment of the gospel of peace; besides all these, taking the shield of faith, with which you can quench all the flaming darts of the evil one. And take the helmet of salvation, and the sword of the Spirit, which is the word of God.

EPHESIANS 6:10-17, RSV

All of this imagery of helmets, breastplates, and special shoes may sound more like instruction of an astronaut going out for a space walk, or a diver heading for the bottom of the ocean, than like an instruction of believers. But it expresses quite clearly two of Saint Paul's main themes: that the Christian is called to a battle between good and evil, and that God provides the resources for that battle. Paul tells us that we live in a hostile environment and an evil time. We are summoned to go out to battle, and we need protection.

These ideas may at first seem to be alien, holdovers from some other age. For most of us, most of the time, everyday life is confined to just the everyday. We go to work, live with our families or our communities, and go about our business. We have our problems, but most of them are problems like fixing the furnace or finding the money for the dentist or trying to make up a quarrel with a neighbor — two-dimensional problems, within our range, manageable. But Paul is telling us here that there is more to our lives and our world than that. We are *not* contending just against flesh and blood, against poverty and disease and personality quirks. There is a spiritual world very closely interwoven with our everyday one — the principalities and powers — and our little struggles have a third dimension, a much bigger and more important one than we usually realize.

Also, Paul tells us that this spiritual world is not all good or even all neutral. There is real spiritual evil out there, and it's "out to get us." The "spiritual" is not necessarily either good or friendly. There are fallen angels as well as good ones. This is an uncomfortable idea. But it certainly accounts for the dark side of reality, the shadow, the evil that we glimpse now and then in our own lives and that seems to appear all too often in the daily headlines. So isn't Paul's image of the adventure, the war, the hero going forth to slay the dragon, true to our experience? Jesus taught us to pray "Deliver us from *evil.*" So Saint Paul here likens the Christian to an adventurer or a soldier girding himself for active service.

In fact, it also sounds rather as though he is talking about Jesus going out into the desert and about the Christian disciple following him. The desert, the wilderness, is the place where most things are absent — shelter, water, food; other people, supermarkets, television. It is a dangerous enough place even on the natural level — hot, dry, barren, full of scorpions and snakes and the "wild beasts" that Mark mentions in his account (1:12-13). But going into the desert also means being alone with yourself, your thoughts, and whatever else may be out there. Here, often enough, there be dragons, as the old maps said. Most people have some shadows and gremlins in their inner spaces. There are two kinds of "gremlins" here, often confused though actually quite distinct: the natural "shadow" of the psyche, and the other spiritual beings that may attack from outside. The natural shadow needs to be recognized, redeemed, and integrated as part of one's mental health and maturity. One would be wise to acquire some measure of discipline on this level before challenging Satan; and even on the natural level, discipline is God's gift and the work of grace.

What Jesus shows by his example, and what Paul too warns us about, is that solitude means being alone, not only with ourselves but with spiritual powers, and with spiritual powers at war. Jesus experienced temptations so deep that the rest of us can scarcely grasp them. Many of the saints and masters of the spiritual life have wrestled with these powers of evil as well. All of us are involved in the war to some degree, though probably not everyone is called to battle these powers directly. When I am tempted to do something I shouldn't — or not to do something I should — this is not always just my own weakness. Some of it at least may be the Evil One actively trying to turn me aside from God. Yes, I remain responsible for my own falls. But another power is at work as well. That is why I need to ask for God's help and use all the resources he gives me.

C. S. Lewis's rendering of this hostile world and of the "rulers of the darkness of this world" is unforgettable. His *Screwtape Letters* is a classic, and very uncomfortable, account of the workings of temptation.[1] His science-fiction trilogy — *Out of the Silent Planet, Perelandra,* and *That Hideous Strength* — is about exactly this spiritual warfare. These stories are dramatic and pictorially vivid. They would make memorable movies if they could be handled well. Lewis calls our earth the *Bent* World, because it has been bent out of its proper

---

1. C. S. Lewis, *The Screwtape Letters* (New York: Macmillan, 1961).

nature, and the *Silent* Planet, because it has lost its proper voice in the music of the spheres. His hero, Elwyn Ransom, is, at least at the beginning of the tale, a quite ordinary university don, suggesting Lewis himself and perhaps modeled partly on J. R. R. Tolkien. Ransom finds himself kidnapped and taken to Mars, where he meets some quite remarkable, quite intelligent, and *unfallen* rational creatures. Later he goes to Venus and meets the Eve of that world just as she encounters the serpent. Ransom also meets the *eldils* — roughly, angels: the spiritual beings who govern the planets. It is they who tell him that the *eldil* of our own earth has become "bent," introducing all the troubles we know. The rest of the trilogy develops this theme. Finally, the third volume returns to earth, bringing the battles of the book of Revelation into an English formal banquet, and the powers of light win a round against the powers of darkness. It's exciting. From one point of view, it's surrealist. From another, it simply describes rather dramatically the same spiritual warfare that all Christians are enrolled to wage.[2]

We ordinary folk live our lives; we go about our daily activities; we make choices. All this talk of battles and spiritual warfare sounds very melodramatic for our rather humdrum lives. Where are all these battles? As one of Lewis's characters puts it, "It may have occurred to you to wonder how any man in his senses thinks we're going to defeat a powerful conspiracy by sitting here growing winter vegetables and training performing bears"[3] — or teaching algebra or selling shoes. But that is just the point. Our little choices are, at least often, part of the spiritual warfare. God and his angels, and also the powers of evil, care how we choose, because our choices are part of that greater war. We are given the choice between God and that "bent eldil," and the choices we make promote the kingdom of one or the other. If I choose to tell a lie, choose to betray a friend, choose *not* to speak up for the right when it might cost me something, I am siding with that bent eldil and promoting his cause.

2. C. S. Lewis, *Out of the Silent Planet* (New York: Macmillan, 1944); *Perelandra* (New York: Macmillan, 1944); *That Hideous Strength* (New York: Macmillan, 1946). The three volumes were first published in England.

3. Lewis, *That Hideous Strength*, p. 221.

Jesus, encountering Satan in the desert, faced some very fundamental choices and met them squarely: food or obedience, power or the Word of God, worship of the true God or worship of a lie. The power of evil was there, active, pressing him to reject his Father's will. Jesus was just as human as we are, and he felt these temptations as strongly as we do, and even more strongly because he had never sinned. But he stood fast and continued to choose his Father's will. He had put on the whole armor of God, and he stood fast. From one point of view, that armor was simply his knowledge of the Scriptures. Each time Satan held out a tempting offer, Jesus replied with the word of his Father, straight from the Bible. Knowing the Bible thoroughly was Jesus' first line of defense against temptation. Paul suggests that it should also be that of every Christian.

Paul tells us to put on the *whole* armor of God. What is this armor? We have just called the Bible and a thorough knowledge of the Bible part of that armor. Paul lists its pieces: truth, faith, and righteousness as our defense, the "sword of the Spirit, which is the word of God" as our offensive weapon. We are given primarily defensive armor because we do not have to win a war on our own. Christ has already won the victory that really matters. It is our job just to remain united to him.

How do we put on that armor? Knowledge is acquired by study; knowledge of God, by study and prayer, study in the spirit of prayer. The disciplines of regular prayer, of times of retreat, of silence and fasting all foster this knowledge. This is no mere academic knowledge in the head; it means knowledge lived out and applied in daily action.

Note the pieces of armor, beginning with truth. Truth matters. Today's world likes to think that everything is relative. But the fact remains that some statements are true, some false, and simply holding to this is part of our faithfulness. The whole process of "discernment" is important precisely because there is an objective truth to be discerned. Somewhere in the fog of our confusions there is the light of God; there are hard facts and certain principles. As we seek to grow in purity of heart, steep ourselves in the Christian tradition, and seek the advice of wise friends, we can learn to see this light and to make our decisions in the context of those principles. These decisions are still fallible, but we must do what we can to ground them in the truth.

I taught high-school math for some years, and I used to wonder what this had to do with serving the Kingdom. But it does relate. Somewhere along the line each of us has to learn that there are given, objective truths we can't weasel around, and math is an excellent place to do this. The multiplication table and the Pythagorean theorem remain true, whether or not I like or even understand them. And truth in daily life matters: if you're a lawyer, a journalist, a real-estate saleman, there will be many times when a lie, a half-lie, a not-quite truth will come in very handy indeed — you might sell that house if you tell the customer the basement doesn't leak. When someone else tries to trap me with a lie, I must meet it with truth. When I am tempted to lie myself, let me "gird" myself with God's truthfulness, just as Paul says.

Next, faith is our shield. How much we need it! How much of my anger, my impatience, my frustration, my depression is the result of not really trusting God, not really believing that God is, and loves, and will make all things well? Can I learn to have the faith to believe that I lost that job, didn't get into that school, failed in that relationship because God has something better in store? Can I accept pain and failure as part of God's love for me? As we learn to have faith in God, then we gradually learn, first, to believe that these sufferings "fit in," and then actually to give thanks for them as part of God's redemptive work. If I really, *really* believed in God, who makes all things work together for good for those who love him, nine-tenths of my surface worries and resentments would just go away. Christ and his saints have not been spared pain, but they have come to have that pain transfigured in the light of the Resurrection. What strengthens faith? Prayer, Bible study, sacraments, Christian fellowship.

Righteousness is our breastplate. Just as there are objective truths, so there are objective standards of right and wrong. "The heart of your word is truth; all your righteous judgments endure for evermore" (Ps. 119:160). Certainly the pastor today needs to be sensitive to circumstances and difficult situations. Nevertheless, the Christian simply is not free to say that "everything is relative." It can be risky and a temptation to pride to say "That is *wrong*," and one is likely to be called "judgmental" or worse, but sometimes it must be done, in humility and trepidation. Faith, love, and charity remain virtues, and hatred, murder, theft, and their kin remain sins. "Doing right" is important not only for its own sake but because it protects us from the attack of evil the next time. Have I trained my conscience so well that it simply won't let me agree to a shady deal, won't let me cheat someone or take something that isn't mine? (Of course the devil doesn't want you to think it's "stealing" — that bald label would give his game away. Circumlocutions and excuses and fancy names work so much better.)

Our one active weapon is the sword of the Spirit, which is the Word of God. Of course this Word is Jesus himself. It is also his Word in the Scriptures. We remember that Jesus defeats Satan by quoting Scripture against him: "Man shall not live by bread alone, but by every word that proceeds from the mouth of God." "You shall not tempt the Lord your God." "You shall worship the Lord your God, and him only shall you serve." (See Matt. 4:4-10; Deut. 8:3; 6:16; 6:13.) The better we know our Bibles, the more deeply the Word has entered into us, and the stronger we shall be when the Evil One or one of his servants attacks us, tempts us, tries to lure us astray. "Oh, come on, try it; it's not all that bad." "But the Lord says. . . ." Jesus here quotes from Deuteronomy. But the whole Bible, Old and New Testaments both, is full of counsel, of strength, of quick answers we can give to Satan. Our text from Ephesians suggests a similar passage in Proverbs: "For the Lord gives wisdom; from his mouth come knowledge and understanding; he stores up sound wisdom for the upright; he is a shield to those who walk in integrity" (2:6-7). The Name of Jesus himself is itself a weapon in our armory: "Whatever you do, in word or deed, do everything in the name of the Lord Jesus" (Col. 3:17). And if you can't do it in his name, don't do it.

This sword of the Spirit is especially part of the armor of the preacher, the teacher, anyone who is called to minister to others in the name of Christ. And isn't that all of us, at least sometimes? When I attempt to help someone else with a problem, when I seek to share a little of what God has given me, I need to be sure that what I'm offering is the Word of God and not some fancy substitute I've thought up for myself.

That is one reason why a life of ongoing prayer relates so directly to a life of Christian action. To minister the Word of God, we must ourselves be steeped in the Word of God. That will require the discipline of regular prayer and regular study to broaden our vision, to strengthen our faith, to see our ordinariness as it really is in the light of the great choices between good and evil. And then to allow our God to fill us with his Holy Spirit and his protection, to provide us with armor against that Evil One who prowls about, seeking whom he may devour — "resist him, firm in your faith," Saint Peter tells us (1 Pet. 5:8-9).

There is another part of the soldier's equipment that Paul doesn't mention in this particular passage, but it also is indispensable, and considering it will help round out our reflections in a very positive way. That equipment is — lunch. We won't get far without it. We need not only weapons, not only truth and guidance, but also strength. Jesus in the wilderness points us to this truth too: "Man shall not live by bread alone, but by every word that proceeds from the mouth of God" (Matt. 4:4). Jewish tradition in fact identified the Word of God with the manna given to the people in the desert. Jesus fasted from the bread of this world, but — or therefore — he was nourished by the true Bread of the Word of his Father. His meat and drink is to do the will of him who sent him. True to this understanding of human nature, God gives us not only his teaching but his strength as well.

Since God has made us creatures of both body and spirit, he strengthens us in both body and spirit. That is, he deals with us sacramentally, as sacramental beings. The world may try to tell us we are *only* embodied beings. Comfort, ease, material things are all that matter. Make sure you have your own comforts, and, if you want to help someone else, look after his material needs, and you've done it all. Command these stones that they be made bread. Sometimes the Church too falls into this trap. Our faith in the Gospel should overflow into running soup kitchens; instead, we sometimes provide the soup and forget the Gospel. Then, on the other hand, some of today's so-called wisdoms will try to deny that our bodies matter at all: think lofty thoughts and never mind the soup kitchen. This is Gnosticism, not Christianity. "Spirituality" is very fashionable, but it isn't always Christian spirituality.

Here, as so often, the true Christian answer is a both/and. We are embodied; the flesh matters; the things of this world matter. But they aren't everything: man shall not live by bread alone. This doubleness of ours, body and spirit, wonderfully and inextricably interrelated, is the principle of the sacraments, and is the reason why God deals with us through the sacraments he has given us. The coming of Christ into the world is itself the greatest sacrament and the principle of all the others. God did not just speak, not just teach. He *came*. Since the first Christmas, the way to know God is to see him, touch him, and know him in Jesus Christ.

So God brings a new Christian into the family of the Church not just by signing him up in the register but by baptizing him with the water of the new birth. I can tell God I'm sorry for a sin, and he will forgive me. But he also gives me a chance to get an outward assurance of his forgiveness; I can confess my sin in the presence of a priest, and God through his priest will pronounce my forgiveness in words I can hear with my own ears. Above all, God not only strengthens our spirits but gives us his own life in the Blessed Sacrament. He strengthens us in body and in spirit through the Bread of Life, which is his Body, through the Sacrament of his Body and Blood. Faithfulness to Christ in the Holy Communion is one of the very best ways of remaining close to our Lord and being strong with him to endure temptation.

Thus God not only calls us to a war but also provides us with the equipment for that war. The Word of God, the Word that is the Logos, Jesus himself, is given to Christian soldiers on earth through the written Word and through the gifts of God's grace. The armor is adapted to the needs of each. Each one is to march out to do battle with whatever particular enemies are in his path, in God's strength and not his own. Then all may come together to know the power of Christ's resurrection.

6 Two Advent Meditations

CHRIST, THE LIGHT OF THE WORLD ─────────────

> The people who walked in darkness have seen a great light;
> those who dwelt in a land of deep darkness, on them has
> light shined.
>
> ISAIAH 9:2

Recently I had the privilege of leading a retreat at Barry House, the conference center of the Diocese of Albany, in the Adirondacks. The chapel there is very simple, very open, and full of windows, and bears an unusual dedication — "to Christ the Light" — with a lovely icon of that theme in the narthex. This could of course be simply natural romanticism, but I think it is a good deal more than that. The theme of light, and especially of light overcoming darkness, is a fundamental theme of the Gospel, and of both Christmas and Easter. The Easter Vigil begins in the dark, with the lighting of the New Fire. The Advent liturgy is full of light, of the promise of light, of light overcoming the dark; and of course by tradition Christ, himself the true Light of the world, was born "when half-spent was the night."

Once upon a time there was a discussion group on family life and the problems thereof. A young mother asked, "How come, every afternoon about five o'clock, the whole household falls apart?" Everyone looked blank for a minute, and then someone ventured, "Because we're all afraid of the dark." A babble of denial broke out, but on reflection many of the group had to admit that on some level they too knew this "childish" fear.

Well, perhaps we *are* all afraid of the dark. I don't know. But I do know that December is a hard time for many people. There is plenty of darkness in our world, natural and supernatural, and in these winter months I suppose we are especially aware of it. With our modern technology we can dispel the physical darkness with the flick of a switch and so escape its real impact, but the mental and spiritual darkness is less easy to evade. In the Church's wisdom, this season of short gray days and long dark nights coincides with her season of Advent and its theme, one among many, of darkness and light. At this season the theme of light calls us to reflect on the coming of Christ, the true Light, into the darkness of the world's night.

The cycle of our Western Christian liturgy was formed in a different time, when the darkness was simple and natural, and some Christian instinct knew to attach the birth of Christ, the dawn of the true Light, to the winter solstice and the pagan festival of the sun. (I wouldn't know quite how to keep my symbolism straight in the Southern Hemisphere.) Today's darkness seems a little more complicated, and we hide from it in our cities with our dazzling artificial lights and our frenetic round of activities. But it's still dark when we get home in winter, and often it's dark most of the day, and it's cold, and Advent remains as a sign, a sacramental sort of season, speaking to us on many levels, of the darkness that is in the world and of the promise of light to come into the darkness.

There are, I suppose, several kinds of darkness. The darkness we find ourselves in can be personal and psychological, or it can be the darkness of sin, or it can be the confusion of our world. Some of this we can change, or at least work on, and we should: we can try to get our own sickness healed, and surely we must repent if the darkness is due to our own, recognized sin. But that leaves a lot we can't do much about, much of it the chaos of the world around us.

There are two ways of being in this kind of dark, and they are poles apart. You can be in the dark, period — no light, no idea that there is such a thing as light. This is fear, despair, alienation, lostness. For the primitive I suppose that night, winter, could bring this kind of fear, because he'd have no assurance the sun would ever return. Today we know that the astronomical light will return, the light of this world — but there's lots of that fear and despair around on other levels, isn't there? Maybe we have even known its shadows in our own hearts. This darkness is the darkness of death, the loss of faith. It is the denial of the Light of the world, refusing to acknowledge that the Light of Christ shines even in the darkness. This absolute darkness is too frightening for most of us to cope with. So we — and, I think, very much our society today — try to escape it by denying it, by turning on all the artificial lights to disguise the emptiness and the darkness.

But the second way to face the darkness is a much more vital and creative thing. This is the acceptance of darkness which knows that the light will return and will prevail, which knows even that the darkness is *necessary* for the light to return. This kind of darkness, this kind of death, is fertile and carries the promise of hope and life. That doesn't make it any less dark while it lasts, or any less painful, or the death, on whatever level, any less real. But there is deep inside it a seed of faith and a willingness to wait and hope and trust in the power of God — and the morning will come in due time, in God's own due time, not ours.[1] This makes of the darkness of death a seedbed for life, as Christ said: "unless the grain of wheat falls in the ground and dies . . ." (John 12:24).

This seems at first glance a strange sort of symbolism for a Christian, and besides that, it's complicated and contradictory. We're supposed to be children of light. So then why all this darkness stuff? As Christians, why do we have to think about it? What's going

---

1. This "prayer of darkness" is of course simply one way of looking at a whole spiritual tradition, that of apophatic, or negative, mysticism. One particularly well-known modern introduction is in T. S. Eliot's *East Coker*:

I said to my soul, be still, and let the dark come upon you
Which shall be the darkness of God.

on here? I think this is where the full Christian message, the true message of Advent, *is* complicated and ambivalent, and is much more true, and much more saving, than any of the simplistic alternatives. We do live, don't we, in a "between" time, a time of both darkness and light. Isn't this true to your experience? We have glimmerings of hope and healing and salvation, we know at least a little of God's amazing grace, but there still seems to be a lot of darkness and evil and suffering around. I see it in me, in the world around me ... and God's amazing grace certainly hasn't finished its work in me. "Beloved, now are we the children of God, and it does not yet appear what we shall be" (1 John 3:2).

The alternatives are simple and simplistic. On one side, the world, the secular society, lives without any real hope, and either abandons itself to darkness or denies the darkness by escape into a frivolous pseudo-light. Don't we see plenty of this everywhere we look? The world's only acknowledgment of Advent, sad to say, is a so-called Advent calendar that teaches a child to count his hoped-for Christmas presents! Sad, and tinselly, and trivial — and so empty. But we can be tempted to embrace an opposite simplicity: I've heard of churches where it's always Easter or Christmas but never Lent or Advent, as if everything were finished and there were no darkness left. But we do not yet see all things put in subjection under our Lord Christ. We are still waiting, working in the between time, waiting for the fullness of the glory that shall be revealed.

You can't do anything to hasten the sunrise or the coming of spring. Switching on the lights just isn't the same. One of the realities about this kind of darkness is that *we* can't fix it. We can only wait in patience for God to fix it, for God to bring his light in his own time into the darkness. Yes, he has done this. In the beginning God created the light. In the fullness of time he sent his only Son, himself the Light of the World, into that world to bring light to those who sat in darkness and the shadow of death. In the end time he will bring in the fullness of his light, and "there shall be no more night there," for "the city has no need of sun or moon to shine upon it, for the glory of God is its light, and its lamp is the Lamb" (Rev. 21:25, 23). But meanwhile we are in the between time, and we have seen the light, but we can only wait for the fullness of light as those who watch for the morning.

Patience, waiting, and acceptance are not easy lessons for modern folks. But they are some of the lessons of Advent, and if we can learn even a little of them, and can wait upon the Lord, our Advent will have been well spent.

A couple of years ago the Lord sent us at our convent in Peekskill a first-class, gift-wrapped lesson in just this kind of waiting. We had our regular Advent retreat scheduled and a full house of people coming for it. The Friday of that weekend, there arrived that winter's great northeaster. Every one of the scheduled retreatants got there, by hook or by crook. But the conductor didn't — no one could get off Long Island. So our retreatants were left to share in the wonderful Advent liturgy with the Sisters, and watch the snow come down, and wait upon the Lord. And they all said it was a most fruitful retreat. Isn't that our image for this season? We listen to God's Word, with its promises of light, and we lay aside our preoccupations and wait for him to speak to us, and to bring the light of dawning day in his own good time.

At this season, those of us who are privileged to pray the daily Offices have our minds full of Isaiah, full of the promises of the light and the dawn. "O Dayspring, brightness of the Light everlasting, and Sun of righteousness: come and enlighten them that sit in darkness and the shadow of death." And every day of our lives we remember the coming of light in the Incarnation and pray for the fullness of the final light in the *Benedictus:* "In the tender compassion of our God the dawn from on high shall break upon us, to shine on those who dwell in darkness and the shadow of death, and to guide our feet into the way of peace" (Luke 1).

May God in his mercy teach us to trust him in the darkness, to wait for the coming of his Light, and to work with him in faith for the kindling of that Light in the darkness of the world.

THE GREAT "O" ANTIPHONS ───────────────

Advent, the season of coming, the season of looking to Christ's coming, is about many things. It is about light coming into darkness; it is about the sanctification of time; it is about patience and waiting; it is about hope and desire; it is about our deepest needs, and about the sure promises of God. It is certainly much more about what God does and what God will do than about anything we can do on our own. I myself cannot think "Advent" for very long without thinking about light, about light in the darkness of my life. I also find its theme of waiting a fruitful one for prayer, of waiting with the old Israel for the promised Messiah, of waiting with our Lady for the birth of her promised Child, of waiting in my own life for God to show me his way, his promises, himself.

The liturgy in Advent weaves back and forth among these themes, and it weaves them together into a single whole. Perhaps they come to their sharpest focus in the so-called Great Antiphons, or the "Great O's." In the traditional monastic Office, these are used as antiphons with the canticle *Magnificat* at Vespers, Evensong, on the last days before Christmas. They are also the basis of the haunting, minor-key hymn "O Come, O Come, Emmanuel," often appearing in Christmas collections but really belonging to Advent instead.

These eight antiphons come from an age very different from ours, and yet they can speak to us with a special poignancy. They were composed sometime in the so-called Dark Ages, perhaps the ninth century, when the lights in Europe burned about as low as they ever have. Somewhere in Europe a monk in his monastery — and monasteries were about the brightest points of light in that dark world — ruminated on his knowledge of Scripture and wove together all the promises of the Messiah into these brief and fervent prayers. They sum up God's promises, asking for the fulfillment of those promises not only in the birth of the Messiah but also in the final consummation of all things. The same special plainsong melody is used for all eight, uniting them even more closely. There is material here for meditation for many Advents.

The very first one, *O Sapientia,* is a prayer for wisdom: "O Wisdom, which came out of the mouth of the Most High, and reaches from one end to another, mightily and sweetly ordering all things: come and teach us the way of prudence."[2]

The Scripture reference here is to the book of Wisdom, and to that personified Wisdom who is the Logos, the Word of God. That makes this prayer explicitly Christian, a prayer to the Lord Jesus Christ himself, begging him to come. Yet his wisdom is already present from the beginning of Creation. It is he who orders all things "mightily and sweetly," whose wisdom planned this world from the beginning, who knows both the convolutions of our history and the glorious final consummation he has planned for it. Doesn't this sum up all the promises of the prophets, that God is in charge of his Creation, that he has planned it all — including our freedom to co-operate with him if we will, or that terrible freedom to refuse him? That not only will he send his Word into the world as its Savior, and that he has done so, but that his Wisdom is with us in this "between" time, while we know God's presence and power and yet do not yet see all things subject to him?

This prayer to the eternal Wisdom addresses, it seems to me, two of our deep human needs and promises to satisfy them. One is the need for meaning, for assurance that there is a purpose to it all — that God our Lord really is in charge and will make all things well. The second is smaller, more intimate — the need for guidance, light, prudence in our own lives, in our perplexities and uncertainties, in making our choices and decisions. We are praying here for God's light and truth in both of these ways.

We live here between his first coming at Bethlehem and his final coming on the clouds of heaven. And we know that his wisdom, his personal Wisdom who is his eternal Son, is in charge of all, even in our own confusion and perplexity. So God's Wisdom encompasses the image of him as light, of light in darkness showing us the way to go, and of power, for he both mightily and sweetly orders all things. He accomplishes his purposes, and we can trust him to do so.

2. The translation of this and the following antiphons is taken from *The Monastic Diurnal Revised*, edited by the Community of St. Mary, Eastern Province (Peekskill, N.Y., 1989), pp. 283-92.

"Come and teach us the way of prudence." Each of these antiphons ends with an urgent prayer, Come — come, Lord Jesus, do as you have promised. Here, come and teach us. Later we will ask for power and strength; here we are asking for guidance, for wisdom in living our lives. For prudence — not at all a colorless word, but, the dictionary says, another word for Providence. Teach us to live by your providence. Teach us to live prudently, wisely, in our personal lives, in our corporate life in the Church, in our life in society. May it be your wisdom that directs us, your light that enlightens us, your hand that guides us — so that we may trust your wisdom and your purpose for the world, and so that we may take our place in that purpose, filled with your wisdom, your truth, your light.

The second antiphon prays, "O Key of David, and Scepter of the house of Israel, that opens and no man can shut, and shuts and no man can open: come, and bring the prisoners out of the prison-house, them that sit in darkness and the shadow of death."

This one is much stronger. First we prayed for wisdom, for light and guidance. Now we are praying for deliverance, for God to come and lead us out of prison. The image, mostly from Isaiah, is complicated. The key is an all-powerful one. If God opens a door with this key, then it is open, and no one can shut it. The gate of heaven, the way to eternal life, is open, and no one can stop us from entering in if we only will. As in Revelation, "I have set before you an open door." And the door it locks cannot be opened: so the way of sin and the power of Satan have been locked away. And what is this key? I suppose the medievals, with their love of allegory, would say the key is the Cross; and that fits, doesn't it?

Sometimes I almost wish it were this easy and find that it isn't: the problem is that there are doors I think are open, and yet I still can't quite manage them, and there are doors I think I have shut on some temptation, and yet the snake still sneaks through them. Do you know what I mean? So while God certainly gives us our freedom, he also really does open some doors and closes others. The important ones have been dealt with. And in our individual lives too: it's sometimes said that God never closes one door without opening another. Sometimes he closes a particular door very firmly — a job, a relationship. If he has shut it, it's shut. Then we have to look for the one he has opened. This one prayer, taken in isolation, sounds almost as if we were asking God to take away our freedom — to force us into the right path by taking away our choices. But I don't think it can really mean that. It's more a part of "lead us not into temptation": please close the doors you know are too much for us to deal with, and open the ones you know we need. Then, as we have prayed before, please give us the wisdom to walk along this path of closed and open doors and to live prudently in this present world.

But then the rest of the antiphon is even stronger. "Come, and bring the prisoners out of the prison-house, them that sit in darkness and the shadow of death." This image always makes me think of Plato's cave — the inhabitants sitting inside watching shadows cast by the fire, when they could be outdoors in the sun. But it's a biblical image too. We are indeed prisoners, not so much of the body and the created order, as Plato probably was thinking, as of confusion and doubt and sin, especially our own — and the valley of the shadow of death is not our permanent home. Another picture here belongs to the Easter mystery: the picture of the Lord Christ on Holy Saturday descending into hell to seek out Adam and Eve and bring them forth with him into the light of his resurrection. Lord God, it is all very well for us to ask you to guide and teach us. But that isn't enough. Some things you will have to save us from by a strong hand, save us in spite of ourselves, grab us by the coat collar and bring us into your new kingdom. Come and deliver us.

And that leads right into the summing-up antiphon: "O Emmanuel, our King and Lawgiver, the Desire of all nations and their salvation: come and save us, O Lord our God."

Emmanuel, God with us. This is our deepest desire, our deepest need, and includes all the others. If God is with us, even in the darkness, we have all we need. And this is the desire not only of Israel but of all nations; and the fulfillment of this desire is our salvation.

We of the Christian dispensation know that the coming of God, the presence of Emmanuel, is a coming in stages. There is the first coming, the coming in the Incarnation, which the prophets look to, that is the obvious meaning of Advent and of our preparations for Christmas. And there is the final coming, the wrapping up of all things at the end of time. It is really this final fulfillment we are praying for, isn't it? Thy kingdom come; even so, come, Lord Jesus. The first Christians really seem to have thought this would come in their own lifetimes. We of the following generations have had to learn that apparently that wasn't what God meant. So there is the in-between time in which we live, when the Lord has come and is here with us, Jesus our Emmanuel, and yet he is still to come. Each year, Advent is given us to remind us of this coming, to teach us to wait and to pray and to long for his coming. May we seek him, prepare for him — in these days of Advent, in our Christmas communions, in the ways in which he comes in each of our lives. Even so, come, Lord Jesus, be Emmanuel, be God-with-us. Be light and wisdom in our darkness; be strength in our weakness. Set our lives in order and increase our longing for your coming. "O Emmanuel, O Emmanuel, our King and Lawgiver, the Desire of all nations and their salvation: Come and save us, O Lord our God."

The Great O's

O Wisdom, which came out of the mouth of the Most High, and reaches from one end to another, mightily and sweetly ordering all things: come and teach us the way of prudence.

O Adonai, and Leader of the house of Israel, who appeared in the bush to Moses in a flame of fire, and gave him the law in Sinai: come and redeem us with an outstretched arm.

O Root of Jesse, which stands for an ensign of the people, at whom kings shall shut their mouths, and whom the Gentiles shall seek: come and deliver us, and tarry not.

O Key of David, and Scepter of the house of Israel, that opens and no man can shut, and shuts and no man can open: come and bring the prisoners out of the prison-house, them that sit in darkness and the shadow of death.

O Day-spring, Brightness of the light everlasting, and Sun of righteousness: come and enlighten them that sit in darkness and the shadow of death.

O King of nations and their desire; the Cornerstone, who makes them both one: come and save mankind, whom you formed of clay.

O Emmanuel, our King and Lawgiver, the Desire of all nations and their salvation: come and save us, O Lord our God.

O Virgin of virgins, how shall this be? for neither before you was any seen like you, nor shall there be after. Daughters of Jerusalem, why marvel at me? The thing which you behold is a divine mystery.

7 Christmas in Lent

From a homily for the Feast of the Annunciation given at the
Church of St. Mary the Virgin, New York City

O n this Feast of the Annunciation to the Blessed Virgin Mary,
we celebrate the Incarnation of our Lord Jesus Christ, the
coming of the eternal into time. So we are celebrating in a hidden
way what becomes manifest to all at Christmas. So today is, to the
eyes of faith, Christmas Day. Today is also a weekday in the middle
of Lent.

Now surely Christmas in the middle of Lent is a paradox. What
do we do about it? Ignore a feast day, a major feast day of our salvation, because it "happens" to fall in a season of penitence? Or do we
"turn off" Lent for a day to enjoy the feast? Let us see if we can find a
way to reconcile the paradox.

Superficially we seem to have forgotten Lent, or so our festive
vestments and flowers and music, our gala celebration, would seem
to indicate. Limited creatures that we are, most of us can only think
about one thing at a time, so maybe this is the best way to do it.

But if we look at this paradox and at this mystery of the Incarnation a little more carefully, I think we will find that this paradox

itself opens a window directly into the central mysteries of our faith. The Incarnation is a paradox, and all of Christianity is a paradox, and our life as Christians is in several ways a paradox.

We call this a feast, a celebration, an occasion for thanksgiving. But Mary, the lowly maid of Nazareth — does she see it at first in that light? She is being called to an impossible task for God, one that, so far as she can see now, is going to bring her only trouble, difficulty, and misunderstanding. And although the promise is that she is to bear the promised Messiah, she can at this point have no understanding whatever of what that may mean. So this message from the archangel is to her a call to a dark journey and a hard task. It is in fact a call to the Cross, though of course she does not yet know that, either. What does she say to the angel? I suppose that most of us, however well-meaning, would say, "No, that's too hard for me," or "Let me think about it," or "I think you have the wrong address." Even Mary at first says, "How shall this be?" But then she says, "Behold the handmaid of the Lord." Her obedience is one of the things for which we give thanks today. And soon she will say, "My soul doth magnify the Lord," and call all generations to join in her thanksgiving.

Let us look at this, if we dare, from God's point of view. Is this humble birth from a Jewish peasant girl a great triumph for God? On the face of it, not at all. The eternal Word, though he is in the form of God, empties himself and takes the form of a servant and becomes obedient unto death, even death on a cross. Here too the Incarnation contains within itself the way of the Cross. And yet it is *therefore* that "God has highly exalted him and bestowed on him the name which is above every name, that at the name of Jesus every knee should bow, in heaven and on earth and under the earth, and every tongue confess that Jesus Christ is Lord, to the glory of God the Father" (Phil. 2:6-11).

So we find in the angel's word to Mary and in Mary's obedience a summary of the Gospel, and we find the paradox of death in life and life in death right at the heart of the feast. The Word becomes flesh and dwells among us; the eternal life is found in our mortal life; earth becomes heaven because it is God's dwelling place. And the incarnate Word takes upon himself not only our flesh but our mortality and the consequence of our sin, and he willingly enters upon the way of the Cross. The glory of God is manifest, and it is manifest most fully in the humility and obedience of our Lord Jesus Christ. The humility and the glory are not two things but one. This is the Christian message, and this is why the message of the Cross is and always has been folly to those who are not prepared to believe.

Our Lady here represents the chosen people of Israel — indeed, she represents the whole human race. She is challenged to accept the awe-ful humility of God and to accept on our behalf the way of the Cross — and she says *Yes*. This is also God's call to each of us, renewed most poignantly in this feast. God calls us to share in his very nature, to receive his divine Life into ourselves. And he calls us to follow him in lowliness, in obedience, in the way of the Cross, which is the way of death before it is the way of resurrection.

All of us are called to work out this same pattern in our own lives. God calls each of us over and over again, often to new and unexpected tasks. Sometimes he calls with a gracious invitation and a promise, and we find out only later that his way is the way of the Cross. At other times, he may ask something that seems totally impossible, with no promise of anything but failure. Either way, every one of us is called to follow Jesus Christ in both his Cross and his Resurrection, and each of us is to say, "I am the Lord's servant; be it unto me according to your word."

Worshiping with you here on Times Square tonight brings vividly to mind a schoolgirl who once stopped in this church to pray, long ago, back in Father Taber's day. She was having one of those arguments with God about one of his calls that we all have had from time to time. God won, as he usually does. But he does have his little jokes: he didn't tell me then, and I could not possibly have guessed, that one element in that call would be that I would someday be climbing into this very pulpit to speak to you.

So what of the paradox expressed in our festal liturgy here tonight? We are indeed celebrating with joy a great feast of our salvation, and we are also truly celebrating it in the shadow of the Cross. The Annunciation contains within itself the way of the Cross. These are not two things, but one. Somewhere I have read an old sermon — by John Donne, I think — for the Feast of the Annunciation falling on Good Friday. Somehow the preacher does hold both of these poles in view. Today we would transfer the feast and not even try to confront the paradox in its full, stark reality. But the truth of that paradox remains, and it is the paradox of the Gospel. The Word has become flesh and dwells among us, and he calls us to follow him, that where he is, there we may also be — in the darkness of Calvary, in the full glory of the Resurrection, and in the life of the world to come.

> *Pour your grace into our hearts, O Lord, that we who have known the Incarnation of your Son Jesus Christ, announced by an angel to the Virgin Mary, may by his cross and passion be brought to the glory of his resurrection; who lives and reigns with you and the Holy Spirit, now and for ever.*[1]

---

1. *The Book of Common Prayer* (New York: Oxford University Press, 1979), p. 240.

8 What Think Ye of Christ?

"What think ye of Christ? Whose son is he?" They said unto
him, "The son of David." . . . But whom say ye that I am?

MATTHEW 22:41

Saint Paul gives us the first Christian confession of faith in the
simple statement "Jesus is Lord" (1 Cor. 12:3), implying that
this expression is not his invention but is already in common use. As
the Church was to discover in several centuries of seeking to understand its faith, this formula can be interpreted on many levels and
can be shown to contain great depths of theological truth. To a
great extent the meaning of this phrase will depend on the context
in which it is used.

The Greek word κύριος, rather like the Spanish *Señor*, is a title
of respect that may be used in several ways. It may mean no more
than a polite "Sir." It may imply a master-servant relationship or, in
New Testament times, a master-slave relationship. But to those
trained in the Jewish Scriptures and conscious of their place in the
covenant community, this term would be first of all the title used in
the Septuagint for the Lord God of Israel. In writing to the Corin-

thians, Paul is probably writing to a mixed gathering of Jewish and Gentile Christians who would be familiar with this Greek version of the Scriptures and who would therefore understand the tremendous assertion being made here. Jesus is being identified with the God of Sinai.

Without its proper context, the assertion "Jesus is Lord" may mean no more than "Jesus is Boss." This is an admirable and succinct statement of personal allegiance, one we may all aspire to say in earnest. But it may mean no more than "This is the captain I choose to follow"; Jesus is considered as one great leader among many others before and after him in many cultures. A Christian today who is unmindful of his historical roots may well suspect no more meaning than this. And, in our highly individualistic society, this same Christian may also be thinking simply of his own individual commitment. He may be quite unaware of the strongly corporate nature of the Lordship of Christ within the Church, like that of the God of Israel in the covenant community of the first Israel.

But when Saint Paul and the early Church are set in their proper context of the Old Testament Scriptures and the self-conscious community of the New Covenant, this title "Kyrios" acquires a theological dimension. "The Lord our God is one Lord" is the creed of Judaism; and in applying this same title to the man Jesus, Paul and the Christian community are asserting that he is God in exactly the same sense that God the Father, the God of Sinai, is God. The Church was to require four centuries of controversy and four major ecumenical councils to come to an understanding of this claim, and even today when we assert its truth, we cannot pretend to grasp its full richness.

In the creeds, our hymns, and all our liturgy, we proclaim regularly just what the Church teaches about the Person of Christ. This teaching proclaims very clearly that the Lord Jesus Christ is truly and fully God, of one Being with the Father; that he is also truly and fully Man, sharing fully in our humanity; and that these two natures are united in his one Person "without confusion, without change, without division, without separation." In December even the supermarkets and street corners blare out these great truths: "God of God, Light of Light, Lo, he abhors not the Virgin's womb; Very God, begotten, not created." "Mild he lays his glory by, born that man no more may die. Ris'n with healing in his wings, light and life to all he brings."

But Christians have never found it easy to hold these truths, and especially not to hold them all at once and to keep them in balance. The great heresies of the fourth and fifth centuries arose when some teacher, or some group of Christians, emphasized one side of the balance to the neglect of the other. Gnosticism and Docetism in all their forms were so absorbed in the divinity of Christ that they were led to deny or to neglect his true humanity. The various schools of Adoptionism and Nestorianism stressed his full human nature, but were led to teach that this man lived so holy a life that he was somehow "promoted" to equality with God, not that he was one with the Father from before all worlds. These two schools of thought are very much with us today, in somewhat different guises and under different names, and neither teaches the full orthodox faith.

It is remarkably easy to hold orthodox beliefs in theory without really grasping their full practical implications. How often do many of us today slide into some form of Adoptionism, assuming that of course Jesus was just like the rest of us, conditioned and bound by his culture, and therefore unable to speak to our very different society? Gnosticism is also prevalent today, though perhaps usually in circles that are only marginally Christian, claiming a "higher truth," a pure spirituality, detached from material and cultural limitations. Curiously, although these two broad types of heresy appear to be completely opposite, they often lead to the same conclusion in practice: that today's Church is free to minimize the authority of the historic Jesus, either because he was merely human and culturally conditioned and didn't understand, or because he is remote from our human condition and has never really been involved in it at all. Either way, history is discounted, and the only source of authority is the Here and Now.

If we seek to claim the fullness of orthodox faith in Christ and to express it for our own time, we are bound, just as our predecessors were, to accept our history and to keep all aspects of our creed in balance. Jesus is Lord: he was, and is, God, fully equal to the Father and Creator. He therefore speaks with authority, both in the Scriptures and within the historic continuity of the Church, the living community that is his witness today. He was, and is, fully human, and the details of his humanity are in some way relevant.

It was God's will to become incarnate in a particular society, that of his chosen people, and at a particular date and place "in the fullness of time." Therefore, his Jewishness, his birth into a patriarchal society founded on a covenant with the Living God, his choice to be male, his choice to be born at a time when Roman rule united the Western world — all these are in some way relevant. It may be appropriate for devotion to portray the Blessed Virgin in the guise of a medieval French princess, or the Nativity in a birchbark lodge somewhere on the Great Lakes,[1] but to take this at all literally would be Gnosticism, denying the reality and importance of the concrete historical facts. If we indeed profess that Jesus is Lord, and with Saint Thomas can say, "My Lord *and my God*," then the whole of Scripture is relevant today, and the whole of Christian tradition as the voice of Jesus within his covenant community is relevant today. We are bound as responsible Christians to use our minds to think, to weigh, to choose, and to interpret, but we are also bound to take very seriously indeed the concrete reality of the Word once and for all made flesh for us and for our salvation. Then in truth we can say, "Blessed is he who comes in the Name of the Lord."

1. *The Hymnal 1982* (New York: The Church Hymnal Corporation, 1982), no. 114.

9 Notes on the Church from Anglican Scholars

Underlying some of the controversial issues in today's Church is the question of the nature of the Church itself, its meaning, its place in God's purpose, and therefore its structure and its way of life. A number of outstanding Anglican thinkers of this century, especially Archbishop Michael Ramsey and Dr. Eric Mascall, have written on these matters, and their teaching can shed considerable light on our present questions. Central to these thinkers is the thoroughly biblical doctrine of the *organic nature of the Church*. While Anglicans have expressed this doctrine in a characteristic way, Christians of other traditions may well find that it fits their own interpretations too. The Old Testament presents God's work as involving primarily the call and formation of a *people;* the New, particularly Saint Paul, speaks of the Church as the *Body* of Christ. The life of this Body and the reason for its existence are in its sharing in the passion and resurrection of the Christ.

Some sixty years ago, an almost unknown young English priest named Arthur Michael Ramsey created a small stir with his first book, *The Gospel and the Catholic Church.* The basic thesis of this book is very simple: that the Gospel and the Church cannot be separated. The Church proclaims the Gospel of Christ's death and resurrection, and the Gospel message itself includes the Church's share in these saving events. "Evangelical" and "Catholic" are terms that should never have come into opposition, because they are necessary complements. This biblical scholar, former Nonconformist and future Catholic-minded Archbishop of Canterbury, develops this theme in thoroughly biblical terms. The remainder of this chapter is based primarily on this book and on a slightly later work, Father Eric Mascall's *Christ, the Christian, and the Church*.[1]

Taking the organic nature of the Church seriously has a number of consequences. First, if the Body that is the Christian Church is the Body of the risen and ascended Lord, then it exists as one whole throughout time. We today are members of the *same* Church as Saint Paul, Saint Augustine, and Saint Anselm, and therefore are their contemporaries and fellow believers, not merely their successors in a temporal institution. Mascall explains it this way:

> The Catholic Church, of which the local church is the manifestation, is not just the Church militant but the whole Church on earth and beyond the grave, militant, expectant, and triumphant. . . . Only too often the Church has been thought of as a purely earthly society, which we enter by baptism and leave by death, a continuing terrestrial organism with a constantly changing membership, comparable in this respect to the Royal College of Surgeons or the Worshipful Company of Fishmongers. . . . The truth, however, is that, although the Church has an earthly part which we call the Church militant, it is not just an earthly reality, and the Church militant at any particular epoch is only a minute fraction of the Church Catholic. . . . Men enter the Church by baptism; they do not leave it by death.[2]

Second, this understanding of the Church means that the Christian Church is one whole and that each of us has a defined place within it. The vocation of an individual is not only his per-

---

1. Arthur Michael Ramsey, *The Gospel and the Catholic Church* (London: Longmans, Green & Co., 1936; reprint, Cambridge, Mass.: Cowley Publications, 1990); Eric L. Mascall, *Christ, the Christian, and the Church* (London: Longmans, Green & Co., 1946).

2. Eric L. Mascall, *The Recovery of Unity* (London: Longmans, Green & Co., 1958), pp. 98-99.

sonal relationship with God ("me and Jesus"), but his place within the Body. It is the Body, the Covenant People, that is called by God and that shares as a whole in the mission, the passion, death, and resurrection of Christ. Ramsey writes,

> The Old Testament itself confronts us with God's method of bringing unity to the human race beset with the disorder of sin. He chooses a nation, and delivers it from bondage, that it may be the instrument of His purpose, a worshipping people who continually praise Him for the acts whereby He has delivered them, and whereby He has kept them in safety. He teaches this people, through painful struggles, to worship him not self-interestedly as a means of securing their own prosperity, but for His own sake, rehearsing His mighty works in creation, in nature, and in history. And Israel has a mission to the nations of the world, who are at last to be drawn into unity with her in the worship of the one God. Thus God proposes to unite mankind through a particular people, and to unite them, not in a programme of philanthropic and social progress, but in the worship of Himself.[3]

In today's culture we are surrounded and influenced by a highly individualistic worldview. But the much broader, much more inclusive, biblical view is that human beings are *not* isolated, autonomous individuals. The human race forms a single whole, and the individual person finds his meaning as a member of that whole. This is the view of both Testaments: Israel is a person, but Israel is also the nation, and often it is hard to be sure which is in view — as, for example, in the Servant Songs of Second Isaiah. Saint Paul's image of the body, in which foot and ear and eye each takes its proper place and is not to be jealous or envious of others, illustrates this eloquently. Thus, to focus on "me" and "my rights" without remembering my place in the Body is less than Christian.

Yet the individual has a real existence and importance, and each Christian in his own person, in his baptism, enters into and re-

3. Ramsey, *The Gospel and the Catholic Church,* p. 20.

lives the passion and resurrection of Christ: "We were buried therefore with him by baptism into death, so that as Christ was raised
from the dead by the glory of the Father, we too might walk in newness of life" (Rom. 6:4). This is why, as Charles Williams points out,
the work of the Church is never finished but has to begin again with
each new generation. This "realist" view of human unity and of
identity, or analogy, on different levels is the biblical pattern, and
the Christian one, and also a curiously modern scientific one. The
old adage of college biology, "ontogeny recapitulates phylogeny"
(the development of the individual parallels that of the species), is
not far from Paul's teaching of our unity in Adam and in Christ.
This is also the classical view. To quote a line from C. S. Lewis's *The
Last Battle*, "It's all in Plato, all in Plato: bless me, what *do* they teach
them at these schools!"

Third, a body has a clear and definite structure. The structure
of the Church, or at least some of the structure, is part of its essential nature, not an optional and expendable extra. One aspect of this
structure is the differentiation of function, the "hand and ear and
eye" of Saint Paul. Differentiation can also imply hierarchy: one person may rightly be "superior" to another by rank and position, as
parent to child or governor to subject, without at all denying their
equal worth as persons before God. A second and more controversial aspect is the teaching, articulated by Mascall, that the historic
ministry of bishops, priests, deacons, and laity is part of the God-
given and permanent order of the Church, not merely one humanly
chosen option among other possibilities:

> If the Church were nothing more than a voluntary association of
> those individual Christians who are now on earth, then its minis-
> try, if necessary at all, might be sufficiently conferred in any way
> that they themselves might contrive. But if the Church is rooted
> in the concrete historical events of the incarnation, death and res-
> urrection of Christ, and if we who are now on earth are only the
> last of sixty or so generations of Christians who have each in turn
> made up the earthly Church, then surely it is most significant
> that the Bishop who exercises the pastoral care and government
> of the faithful in each place has received his commission and his

sacerdotal character not merely from that small and struggling part of the Church which is now militant on earth, but, by a kind of spiritual and sacramental inheritance, from the generations of the past. . . . The Bishop is therefore not merely the organ of the earthly Church, past or present, but of the whole Church of Christ, here and beyond the grave.[4]

If the teaching outlined above is acknowledged as orthodox Anglican — and Catholic — doctrine, then a number of consequences follow. The most obvious is that if the order and structure of the Church are part of God's fundamental revelation, then we had better be very hesitant indeed about venturing to change that order and structure.

There are also some less obvious consequences. The first provides a solution to the dilemma of trying to hold a truth one believes important, such as apostolic succession, without seeming to "unchurch" or condemn or judge those who do not share it. The Church is a single body, and its ministry is a function of the whole. As J. V. Langmead Casserley explains in his book *Christian Community,* "The historic episcopate is essential to the validity of the Church as a whole rather than to the validity of any particular liturgical action engaged in by a number of sincere Christian people."[5] Ramsey continues the point:

> We are led, therefore, to affirm that the Episcopate is of the *esse* of the universal Church; but we must beware of mis-stating the issue. All who are baptized into Christ are members of His Church, and Baptism is the first mark of Churchmanship. Yet the growth of all Christians into the measure of the stature of the fullness of Christ means their growth with all the saints in the unity of the one Body, and of this unity the Episcopate is the expression. It speaks of the incompleteness of every section of a divided Church . . . [and] it proclaims that there is one family of God before and

---

4. Mascall, *Christ, the Christian, and the Church,* pp. 122-23.

5. J. V. Langmead Casserley, *Christian Community* (London: Longmans, Green & Co., 1960), p. 61.

behind them all, and that all die daily in the Body of Him who died and rose.[6]

Martin Thornton's discussion of the "Remnant" in his *Pastoral Theology* applies here. Israel was chosen for a special role, but that role was for the sake of the whole world, and Israel betrayed her mission either when she "intermingled with the heathen and learned their pagan ways" (Ps. 106:35), or when she took pride in her unique role. Similarly, the Church is called for the sake of the whole world and must both preserve her God-given identity and reach out to those presently outside her ranks. She has been entrusted with great gifts, not only for the sake of her present members but for the sake of all human beings. Presumably it is fair to extend this argument by saying that traditional-minded Catholics must be faithful to what they understand as true, while gladly acknowledging God's different gifts to others. Probably all of us are missing something and do not know it: as Mascall comments in *The Recovery of Unity,* "Treasure packed into earthen vessels can acquire a very odd shape."[7]

Two other consequences deal with "relevance." Some thinking Christians might well dismiss this whole discussion as irrelevant and ivory-tower, when the *real* issues of the day lie in social justice and personal spirituality. But please notice how well these pieces fit into our picture. Social issues are important for Christians because they affect the welfare both of the whole Body and of its individual members. Yet a concern for social justice needs to be grounded in an understanding of what the social order is meant to be. Spirituality, if it is Christian, is not an isolated individualism but is rooted in the nature and life of the Church. Disconnected from the common life, it can easily "wander into myth," as Saint Paul warns, or into narcissism; to grow spiritually is to contribute more to the life of the Body. In return, a concern for justice and for spirituality serves to keep theology alive and responsible, lest ecclesiology alone become an end in itself, a "spiky" devotion to a little tin god.

6. Ramsey, *The Gospel and the Catholic Church,* pp. 84-85.
7. Mascall, *The Recovery of Unity,* p. 36.

In this time of confusion and controversy, a remark made by Dr. Casserley in 1960 seems a valid consequence of Archbishop Ramsey's linking of "Catholic" and "Evangelical," and a fitting conclusion to this discussion. While expressed in Anglican terms, it is surely applicable as well outside that fold: "For the moment the essential Anglican rule, upon which we must all insist with equal emphasis, is that nothing should be done by one party or group of Anglicans which would make the position within Anglicanism of any other party untenable. This applies equally both to those evangelicals who are so enthusiastic about the ecumenical movement as to compromise our catholicity and its interests, and to those Anglo-Catholics whose concept of catholicity is so rigid and mistaken as to exclude the evangelical impulse."[8]

And, as Saint Benedict prays, may God bring us all together to eternal life.

8. Casserley, *Christian Community,* pp. 137-38.

IO Community and the Common Life

The Religious Vocation

The three themes of Scripture, liturgy, and community have been constantly interwoven in this book. Community is grounded in Scripture; Scripture is best expressed in liturgy; liturgy is by its very nature the work of the community. This third thread, the one of the Christian Church as the people of God and the archetypal community, has been expressed in many ways. For modern Christians, it may mean the life of a Christian family, and probably for most people first and foremost the common life of their parishes and congregations. Special, short-term communities, such as those formed in youth conferences, Cursillo, and renewal weekends, are often profoundly life-changing experiences for those who take part in them. For some Christians, social concern has led to an active involvement in politics and programs of social change, efforts to embody the Christian vision in the entire society. In a different vein, throughout Christian history longer-term communities, usually "monastic" to a greater or lesser degree, have also arisen as special expressions of the Gospel life.[1]

1. In this context the terms "religious" and "monastic" are used in a technical

74

From one point of view, the "monastic" or "religious" vocation is simply the universal Christian vocation: to love and serve God and neighbor. From the specific point of view of this book, however, a monastic community is a very concrete illustration of retelling and living the Christian story. The backbone of monastic life is the regular recitation of the Divine Office, which involves the continuous reading of the entire biblical story and the daily praying of the Psalms. For modern Anglicans, the rediscovery of the monastic vocation has been one of the fruits of the nineteenth-century Oxford movement; religious orders of various types now serve Anglican churches all over the world.

The "religious" vocation, using the term in its broadest sense, has taken many forms. The present volume comes from a modern American community professing the Benedictine tradition but having its own characteristics as well. Other contemporary Anglican orders are grounded in other traditions. It may be instructive to look first at a very modern, "apostolic," English community that at times in its history has also drawn from the Benedictine tradition, and then to consider the more "monastic" American Community of St. Mary in its recent history, before turning to a consideration of just what this whole tradition can mean for people today.

A religious community, whether an "active" one intensely involved with the surrounding world, or a more "monastic" or "contemplative" one — all of these terms are ambiguous — inevitably exists in a complex and ambivalent relationship with the culture around it. Monasticism is almost by definition marginal to its culture, against or at least apart from the "world," against whatever excesses the spirit of its particular age may endorse. But, also inevitably, a monastic culture in any age also shares in and responds to that age. Its members come to it shaped by their contemporary culture,

---

sense. The "religious" life or vocation, or a "religious" order or community, refers to a life formally professing the vows of poverty, chastity, and obedience, or the equivalent, and a person dedicated to such a life may be called a "religious." The term "monastic" is more specific and refers to a form of the "religious" life that is communal and at least relatively enclosed or separated from the larger society. "Monastic" may be contrasted with "apostolic," referring to a more missionary and socially involved form of the "religious" vocation.

and its service will be directed to the needs of its time and its society. One of the consequences of this influence is that changes in the society will necessarily bring changes in the community's attitudes and ways of service. These two communities both illustrate this interrelationship, each in its own way.

The Community of the Resurrection

The English Community of the Resurrection, "CR," based at Mirfield in Yorkshire, is well known in England and abroad for its training of priests, for its active social and political role in the Anglican Church, and for a number of outstanding individual members such as Bishop Trevor Huddleston. Its inner history has recently become accessible to outsiders through the publication of an extensive centenary history, written by one of its own former students who had full access to private community records.[2] CR has not been obviously "Benedictine" or "Franciscan" or anything else familiar; an American Episcopalian might find some parallels in the Order of the Holy Cross, "OHC." Some years ago, in his life of Raymond Raynes, former Superior of CR, Nicholas Mosley made this observation: "The course of a man's spiritual life is often determined on the human side by the tensions which cannot be resolved within it."[3] This principle was clearly illustrated in Father Raynes's life, as the whole biography goes on to show. It is also in many ways an appropriate theme for the story of his community.

The Community of the Resurrection grew from several roots, one of them the Christian Socialism of the late nineteenth century; this is one of its chief parallels with OHC. Its founder, Charles Gore, was an aristocrat, a theologian, and later a bishop; and, although he is buried at Mirfield and venerated as a founder, he himself actually lived in community only for brief periods. A number of tensions are

2. Alan Wilkinson, *The Community of the Resurrection: A Centenary History* (London: SCM Press Ltd., 1992).

3. Nicholas Mosley, *The Life of Raymond Raynes* (London: The Faith Press, 1961), p. 24.

implicit here: between a genuine concern for social justice and a persisting upper-class ethos; between an "apostolic" and missionary thrust and a more "monastic," contemplative spirit; between the desire for community life and the very strong individualism of many members. As a number of members of CR have become bishops, the issue of "prelate brothers" has been a lively one. The "liberal Catholicism" of Gore has typically been the theology of CR, but for a time in the middle of this century the brethren were identified instead with the rather rigid Anglo-Catholicism (using the term in its narrowest and "spikiest" sense) that was prevalent in some quarters before Vatican II. The community has made a point of its loyalty to the Church of England and has often had the Archbishop of Canterbury as its visitor, but its members have also often been embroiled in various controversies and quite at odds with the "establishment" — as, for example, under Archbishop Randall Davidson.

CR has attracted many very strong men in its hundred years. Charles Gore and Walter Frere, its co-founders, both rank as important theologians, and both became bishops. Edward Keble Talbot, Superior from 1922 to 1940, was much beloved both within and without the community and much in demand as a retreat conductor and spiritual director; he perhaps represents the "monastic" element.[4] Raymond Raynes was Superior from 1943 to 1958 and one of the outstanding leaders of the English Church in those years, although (or perhaps even because) they were a period of great strain within both Church and Community. Trevor Huddleston, who died in 1998, was a principal catalyst for social change in South Africa, a bishop both in Africa and in England, and a formative influence on Desmond Tutu. This galaxy of scholars and leaders hardly seems compatible with a community teaching self-effacement and subordination; yet that too is one of the paradoxes of CR.

The community began work in South Africa in 1903 and is still there, although now only on a limited scale. Its work in education, in the training of priests, and in social action, both in the Union (Sophiatown, Rosettenville) and in Zimbabwe (Penha-

---

4. *Retreat Addresses of Edward Keble Talbot*, ed. Lucy Menzies (London: SPCK, 1954).

longa), has been a very significant force in African Anglicanism, and has also been for many members of CR the primary focus of their vocation. No less than thirteen of them are buried at the remote station of Jane Furse Hospital in the northern Transvaal. Here is still another complex of tensions. The brothers in England and those in South Africa have often lost touch with one another and have not always seen the community vocation in the same light; the community has pioneered in the formation of a multiracial society and yet has attracted few African members; and the issue of political activism, and the degree of involvement appropriate for religious, remains controversial.

Alan Wilkinson, who himself was trained at Mirfield, has written this comprehensive history with full access to inside sources and apparently with encouragement to be perfectly open. He tells his story, so interwoven with Church and (especially in South Africa) with political affairs, fully and honestly. This openness has been characteristic of CR. Its own members have written a good deal, and its *CR Quarterly* continues to be valuable.[5] More recent involvements have been with ecumenical affairs, especially in Romania and other parts of Eastern Europe, and these activities are reported in depth in the Quarterly. It is also typical of this community that the Quarterly provides full and very interesting "warts and all" biographical sketches and obituaries for departed members. The community's own history is in the same tradition: frank, analytic, critical and self-critical, "warts and all," and very much involved in the life of its times.

The Community of St. Mary, 1941-1991

The Community of St. Mary has perhaps been especially sensitive to cultural changes, because it has never been devoted to any one particular work. Founded in New York City in 1865 with the guidance of the Reverend Morgan Dix of Trinity Parish and others, it has

5. *CR Quarterly*, published by the Community of the Resurrection, Mirfield, West Yorkshire, WF14 OBN, England.

engaged in works ranging from middle-class boarding schools to inner-city social work to missions in the Philippine back country. Its 1906 Rule spoke of "all the corporal and spiritual works of mercy of which a woman is capable" — some of us sometimes felt that that seemed to mean all of them at once! But that unrestricted agenda has meant that the sisters in each generation have been able to respond to whatever needs were presented to them, and the style of the community has changed accordingly. The dramatic changes in America in this century — three major wars, television, a baby boom, a revolution in the role of women, and that whole complex called "the Sixties" — have produced corresponding changes in the life of this group of women seeking to serve the Lord. A centennial history of the community was published in 1965,[6] at or near the height of a rather stable period. The fiftieth profession anniversary of two sisters in 1991 provided a convenient reference point to consider the significant changes of the subsequent years. The following essay was written for that occasion and has been updated in a few places to make it current.

From St. Mary's Messenger, May 1941:

"April 25 — The Rev. S. C. Hughson, O.H.C., received the profession of Sister Anastasia and Sister Mary Basil."

This succinct announcement was the entire "press coverage" for two life professions, a significant event in the life of a relatively small community. What else was happening in the Community of St. Mary in 1941? The same "Bi-Monthly Chronicle" records the clothing of two novices (the names are not given, but one was Sister Lioba and the other a novice who later withdrew); two retreats led by Dom Anselm Hughes, O.S.B.; some Associates' news; and a Quiet Day at DeKoven Foundation in Wisconsin for the Junior School girls of Kemper Hall. Articles in the same issue include retreat notes by the Rev. Frank Vernon, the Community's Chaplain General; two letters from the Philippines; an article on St. Macarius the Egyptian;

6. Sister Mary Hilary, CSM, *Ten Decades of Praise* (Racine, Wis.: DeKoven Foundation, 1965).

and an appeal for Bundles for Britain, underscored by two war letters from England.

What was the Community of St. Mary like in 1941? Its work was largely institutional: sisters worked in four schools (St. Mary's, Peekskill, N.Y.; St. Mary's, Sewanee, Tenn.; Kemper Hall, Kenosha, Wis.; St. Katharine's, Davenport, Iowa); St. Mary's Hospital for Children on West 34th Street in New York City's Hell's Kitchen, with a summer location in Norwalk, Connecticut; St. Mary's in the Field, Valhalla, New York, for troubled girls; and St. Mary's Home, Chicago, primarily for orphans. Also, the mission at Sagada in the Philippines was a major interest, and the new native Sisterhood of St. Mary the Virgin was just coming into being. Retreats were given frequently at the Peekskill and Kenosha convents, at DeKoven Foundation (which the Western Province had recently begun to operate), in the summer at St. Raphael's House in Evergreen, Colorado, and sometimes in still other branch houses.

At that time, and for some years later, a new sister entering the community found an established group of works and could expect simply to be assigned to a junior position in one of them. Quite typically, the newly professed Sister Anastasia was sent to work at St. Mary's School, Peekskill, and Sister Mary Basil went to St. Mary's Hospital. Institutional work fitted well with the highly structured life of the community, it met real outside needs, and it was work for which many of the sisters were qualified. Hard work and a good general education were adequate preparation for a wide variety of tasks.

The community was large by Episcopal Church standards, nearly at its largest, with two provinces based respectively in Peekskill and Kenosha, and widely respected. The annual Chapter report for 1941 lists sixty-eight professed members of the Eastern Province alone. The Superiors were Mother Mary Maude, the Mother General; Mother Mary Theodora in the East; and Mother Mary Ambrose in the West. A sister's life was supposed to be anonymous and hidden. There was great stress on avoiding "singularity," although community folklore records a generous number of "characters" over the years. Articles by sisters in the *Messenger* were not signed, and, as we saw above, almost no personal information about any of the sisters appeared in print. When Sister Mercedes published her historical novels for young people (*Father Junipero Serra* was one of the most popular), she used the name Ivy Bolton, with no indication that she was a member of a religious community. The faculty list for St. Mary's School contained entries for "A Sister of St. Mary: Latin" or "A Sister of St. Mary: Physical Science," followed by her credentials, sometimes impressive ones, but not her name. This last policy was changed only when Sister Frideswide became Superior of the school in 1960.

Then, and for perhaps another twenty years, almost everyone took this framework for granted. It is very evident in the centennial history, *Ten Decades of Praise*, published in 1965. It worked, both for the community and for the individual. Novices kept coming; some left as novices, but only rarely did a sister leave after profession (just two of those sixty-eight). The community, with its large body of Associates and friends, was settled, perhaps somewhat aloof, respected, working well internally, and serving the Church and society in a number of recognized ways.

Obviously, a number of things have changed, both without and within the community. The sixties and seventies were a time of change and ferment for religious as well as for everyone else. One important result has been the decentralization of the community. In place of two provinces under a Mother General, trying to be exactly alike in all respects, there are now three autonomous provinces (the third is Sewanee), each expressing quite a different form of the community's original vocation and spirit, all united by a common heritage in spite of some occasionally deep disagreements. (No one who attended the 1969 General Chapter at DeKoven will quickly forget some of those.) Because of this diversity, no one author could speak fairly for all three provinces: the remainder of this discussion will focus on the Eastern Province. The publication of this material in itself illustrates one change, for the community is far less reticent about sharing its experience with others, now seeing its vocation more surely as part of that of the whole Church.

Both outside influences and internal developments have shaped changes in the community's life and mission. As state social services and regulations have expanded, hard work alone, without specialized training, will not run a school or a hospital.

This increasing professionalism became very difficult to combine with a full monastic life. Our schools have been closed, partly for that reason, partly for lack of funds, and St. Mary's in the Field was merged into another similar agency. We withdrew from the Philippines in 1967, as the Philippine Church began moving toward autonomy. (In 1992 the Southern Province re-established the Philippine connection, and the members of the native community were received as professed members of CSM.) St. Mary's Hospital for Children is flourishing, but the sisters' involvement is now almost entirely on the board level. While we are no longer really needed for social services, we have found instead a deep and widespread hunger on a more directly spiritual level. We try to meet this need by providing retreats and quiet days, counseling, a place of prayer, and an extended Christian community. This seems to be important as a "support system" for a remarkably wide range of people, both Associates and many others. Thus, Sister Anastasia, after many years at St. Mary's School and St. Mary's in the Field, is now largely occupied with counseling individuals, letter writing, and prayer. Sister Mary Basil, after working at St. Mary's Hospital and St. Mary's School, served twenty years as Mother of the Eastern Province, and later became Novice Mistress to pass on the tradition to a new generation.

The mission of St. Mary's Hospital for Children and its relation with the community have evolved significantly. The sisters founded the Hospital in New York's Hell's Kitchen in 1870, when treating sick children separately and differently from adults was a radical new idea. At first the sisters did almost all the work themselves, with medical professionals often donating their services. The work was supported by gifts: when Sister Catherine, the Superior for sixty years, needed something, she could ask Mrs. Astor to call with her checkbook. Quite a few things have changed. The hospital was moved to Bayside, Queens, in 1950. A full professional staff is employed at competitive salaries. Financing involves Medicaid, insurance, and managed care, as well as professional fund-raising. But the sick and needy children are still there: at any given time the hospital now serves over a thousand of them, many in their own homes. The gifted, dedicated professionals are still there, and have brought

St. Mary's to a leadership position in the care of children with special health needs. The sisters no longer do the daily work themselves, but their role remains what it always was: to remind everyone that we are all here because the children need us, that we are here to serve them and their families, to reverence them as persons of value, to help to make their lives better. Even when neither child nor caregiver nor supporter is explicitly Christian, the work is still done in the name of the God of love.[7]

At the same time, the community's internal life has changed, though more subtly. Like most other communities, we have seen far fewer vocations, and a considerable number of professed sisters have left since the sixties. Some found their calling in the active works and chose those over community life, while others doubtless were affected by the same forces which have produced divorces and frequent career changes for a whole generation. There are now (1999) ten professed Sisters in the Eastern Province, and another eleven in the South.

In her years as Mother, Sister Mary Basil led the community in a study of its rule and life, discerning essential principles while adapting the expression of them. "CSM East" is today one of the more traditional communities, and this is by considered choice. Mother Miriam, who became Superior in 1996, is one of the younger sisters but was trained largely by Sister Mary Basil. The community has been involved in liturgical renewal since Bishop Albert Stuart asked us to begin trial use of the "green book" in the mid-sixties. Our present usage (we use the 1979 Book of Common Prayer, and prefer Rite II) is very much like that of many parishes — far more in the Episcopal "mainstream" than the old Anglican Missal ever was — but most of us are by no means ready to accept all of the other recent innovations in Church teaching and practice. We thought it important to preserve the monastic Divine Office and the musical work of Canon Winfred Douglas instead of changing to the "Prayer Book Office" with its quite different balance. Accordingly, the sis-

7. This paragraph is based on a talk given by (then) Mother Mary Jean at the St. Mary's Hospital 125th Anniversary Dinner Dance in 1995 — itself an event unimaginable in 1870 or even 1941.

ters put ten years of patient work into producing *The Monastic Diurnal Revised,* published in 1989.

In the common life, there is much more room for, and open expression of, differences in personality and interest. The sisters still wear a traditional habit, but it has been simplified and made washable. They have retained the titles "Sister" and "Mother" that some communities have dropped, but their decision-making is more open and consensual than autocratic. Where formerly the sisters were not supposed to attend "social gatherings outside the houses of the Community, or public meetings whether they be ecclesiastical or not," they now sometimes do so and sometimes even speak at them, although still only selectively. Although several sisters have some form of individual ministry, and each is encouraged to develop her own gifts, the work each does is understood as the work of the whole community. The community is definitely more than a federation of individual projects. This distinction is important and is one reason for calling the community "Benedictine" rather than "Augustinian." We see ourselves today as called to live a Christian community life, nurturing the growth of God's work in persons both within and without the community, serving the Church primarily by prayer and hospitality, open to whatever calls God may have in store for us. If some future sister, now perhaps a toddler, writes a sequel to this essay in the year of grace 2041, we believe that it will show a continuity of God's work in his dealings with us.

Monastic Principles in the Marketplace

Not every Christian is called to the monastic life, and in recent times only a tiny handful have undertaken the celibate community life under vows. But the principles that guide this life have proved over the centuries to be useful and valid for many Christians in other walks of life as well. Someone has said, "All Anglicans are Benedictines." It certainly is true that the Book of Common Prayer and the way of life it envisages are grounded in the long tradition of Benedictine houses in England and are intended to make the essential values of the monastic way of life available to everyone. The bucolic image of the peaceful village with an exquisite stone church as its center seems dated and romantic today; yet, with a little effort, we can identify underlying principles that will be as valid in postmodern America as they were in the late Roman Empire or in pre-industrial England. In these unsettled times a number of books of "convent wisdom" for the general public have been quite popular. Some people have found themselves called to go one step further, to undertake a rule incorporating some of the monastic principles while continuing to follow a "secular" vocation. These people may be called Associates, Oblates, Tertiaries, or something else; the idea is not new, but its role of providing a supporting structure for those outside the "structure" seems to have special meaning today.

I would like to focus here on three "Benedictine" principles,[8] which may be summarized as follows:

- Rule, "regula," gives structure to life.
- Life is a whole: prayer and work belong together.
- Life is communal: we are not isolated individuals.

"Regula" Ties It All Together

Words like "rule" and "regulation" are out of favor today, and even "regulate" suggests either a bureaucracy or a machine. Yet, paradoxically enough, high-powered management experts can command large fees for helping individuals and businesses to "get things organized," and simple items like appointment calendars have become complex and costly leather-bound volumes or equally complex and costly software packages. Benedict of Nursia addressed essentially the same problem in the fifth century and found a much simpler solution in the principle of Rule, *regula*. His first principle is also the one often cited first by those management experts: set your priori-

8. The term "Benedictine" has been used in a variety of ways. In this context it is a shorthand term used for convenience, claiming only that the principles discussed here are grounded in the Rule of Saint Benedict and the tradition based on that Rule.

ties right, and everything else falls into place. This principle will work just as well for Christian life in the twenty-first century as it did in the fifth.

The Benedictine day is organized around the "hours" of the Divine Office, and a large part of the original Rule is devoted to working this out in detail. Prayer is the first work of the monk, and therefore time for prayer — meaning primarily *corporate* prayer — is the first thing scheduled. But the timetable also provides for meals, study, work, and sleep, each equally important at its proper time and all in balance. Benedict was providing a means for handling several different human weaknesses. There is ordinary laziness, the temptation to waste time doing nothing in particular. There is the less easily recognized form of sloth, the habit of getting so engrossed in one thing as to fail to go on to the next at the proper time. In Benedict's time there was also unregulated desert monasticism, where monks competed to see who could say the most Psalms or who could fast the longest. It was his genius to bring this unbridled zeal into order and to establish what he called his "little school of the Lord's service," in which quite ordinary men and women could glorify God in a balanced life.

Modern religious communities have changed the details of Benedict's Rule almost beyond recognition to suit their changed living conditions. Electricity, printing, and the loss of the agrarian society are of course major elements in this change. But at least the more "monastic" communities have retained the principle of an ordered day with corporate worship given priority, and this principle is an important part of their witness to the world. For example, the schoolgirls at St. Mary's School were always astounded to learn that the very first piece placed in the puzzle of making the school schedule was the sisters' chapel times. There might be three or four sisters teaching on a faculty of a dozen or more, but those three or four were *not available* first period or fifth. Worship came first. The girls attended chapel daily themselves, but for some reason this small fact always surprised them.

An ordered day is all very well for a special, small community explicitly dedicated to Christian service. But the same principle can also be very helpful for the ordinary individual Christian in a "secular" calling and environment. Recognizing the important elements in one's life, setting aside time to give each its proper place, and keeping these things in balance — this is another way of "getting organized"; and giving prayer its proper first place does in fact pull all the others together. Of course for most people today a rule, or any timetable, has to be flexible. But "flexible" does not have to mean "flabby." The family that makes a commitment to share dinner together is an excellent example of being willing to put effort into family life. A commitment by an individual or a family to regular times of prayer puts similar effort into the Christian life. This is what a "Rule of Life" means, primarily: a commitment to regular daily prayer and to some regular part in public worship.[9] How much, when, and what kind will vary enormously with personal circumstances. Some people link this commitment to Rule with one of the religious communities by becoming Associates.

Of course, a social worker with a crowded calendar or a busy young working mother cannot keep all the "hours" of the Divine Office and would be most unwise to try. But any Christian who wants to grow in prayer and the knowledge of God will need a commitment to *regular* prayer (prayer according to *Regula!*). That has always meant public worship every Sunday — by long tradition, the Holy Eucharist — and also needs to mean committing time *every day* for personal prayer. Today the "daily prayer" usually has to be done privately, by the individual alone, perhaps at home or during lunch hour or on the bus. But it is still a sharing in the corporate prayer of the whole Church. That is why for most people it should include some share in the Office, the regular and objective reciting of Psalms and other Scriptures and set prayers. One's more private, personal, "devotional" times of prayer or Bible study or reflection are also important and should gradually nurture and grow into an ongoing attention to God in all things, perhaps part of what Paul meant by "prayer without ceasing." Without some more objective prayers to balance these, however, they can easily become both vague and individualistic.

9. For more on the subject of personal Rule, see Martin Thornton, *Pastoral Theology: A Reorientation* (London: SPCK, 1958).

The more objective, set, "Office-type" prayer lifts us to another level, to a sharing with the whole Church, and "with angels and archangels and all the company of heaven," in the recalling of the Christian story and the worship of Almighty God.

Prayer Overflows into Work

Saint Benedict in his Rule lays great stress on the *Opus Dei,* the Work of God, by which he means primarily the community's corporate worship and recitation of the Divine Office. But the term can also be applied to the monastic life as a whole, and that is precisely the point. For the monk — and for that matter, for every Christian — the work that he offers to God and does in the strength God provides is *all* of the work God gives him. Yes, prayer is work, and a life of regular prayer can be very demanding work. But washing dishes or doing accounts or interviewing clients is, or should be, equally God's work. Within the monastery this is relatively simple, if not always easy: times of prayer and times of "work" are both assigned, and both are equally matters of obedience. The principle of *laborare est orare,* "to work is to pray," is capable of several meanings and is more profound than it sometimes appears.

Benedict says, "Regard all the utensils and tools of the monastery as the sacred vessels of the altar." No one work is "better" or "holier" than another. It is not "holier" to be absorbed in prayer in the chapel than to be attending to the convent's guests. It will take most of us a good many years to be able to live this way at all fully, but the principle is clear enough. *Everything* we are given to do can equally be done for God. Again, of course, this is a little simpler in the monastery. But even there the telephone, the broken drainpipe, or the cranky coworker can present a challenge. In a thoroughly secular environment the challenge is much greater: How am I to discern the presence of the Lord Christ in an adversarial courtroom situation, or a deadening stack of data entry, or a mile-long traffic jam? But Benedict has given us the principle. So has Saint Paul: "Whatever you do, in word or deed, do everything in the name of the Lord Jesus" (Col. 3:17).

One popular modern interpretation of *laborare est orare* is misleading and threatens to empty it of content. This is the argument: "To work is to pray. My work is running this soup kitchen, or doing advocacy, or teaching kindergarten. That's my prayer. Therefore, I don't need to 'pray' in any other sense." This is to attempt to solve the dichotomy by abandoning one side of it. It risks, in the language of the Athanasian Symbol, the conversion of the Godhead into flesh rather than the taking of the Manhood into God. Benedict's answer, though he does not use the word, is rather to keep the two kinds of "prayer" in *balance*. In fact, the Christian activists who have done most to change the world, like Mother Teresa and Dorothy Day, have spent long hours in hard work and often equally long hours in contemplative prayer. Prayer and work are complements, not opposites, and both serve the same Lord.

For the person outside the monastic structure, the same principles can apply, but the discernment involved may be much more subtle. How can I give proper time both to prayer and to work? Which takes priority? How do I decide *right now* whether it's more important to say Evening Prayer, when that is something I have promised to do, or to write three letters? One solution to these dilemmas is in the concept of "Rule." Perhaps we could say that prayer-work and work-work (work-prayer?) both have their legitimate place, and a serious Christian will not want to let either entirely displace the other. The trick is to find the right balance, the balance that God wills, for me, now, in this situation.

Life Is Communal

In our individualistic culture, people have often felt isolated and have sought community, ties, and support systems in many places. The Christian Church and, within it, the monastic tradition have a good deal to say to this isolation. As we have seen from the beginning of this work, the Christian story is the story of a *people* and of God's dealings with that people. Christian worship involves the retelling of that common history within the fellowship of the worshiping community. This sense of community is much more than the formation of individual, one-to-one ties of friendship; it asserts that being human means having a place in an entire ordered society. The Church in any one place and time is one embodiment of that society; a monastic community is another, smaller such embodiment.

A community is quite different from a collective. If society is an ordered whole, then each person has a unique place within that whole, and each one has a place to belong. There are no interchangeable parts. No one has to be complete in himself; it is the whole body that is to manifest the "measure of the stature of the fullness of Christ" (Eph. 4:13). I don't have to do everything myself; I have my own gifts to contribute, but I can look to you for those that I lack. There are real differences, and there may well also be real ranks. Some people may well have legitimate authority over others, and one may excel over others in certain areas. But because all are of equal worth, there is — or should be — no room for rivalry or jealousy. Of course we all know that in a fallen world such things do exist, but we seek, as we all are gradually converted and re-formed in the likeness of Christ, a harmonious society where they have been left behind.

Historically, Benedictine monasteries have reflected this principle of complementarity in various ways. The earliest Benedictine abbeys were self-contained medieval estates like others around them, and the monks themselves did most of the work. Later there was more specialization, and the monks became to some extent the "educated" class, while serfs did the work. Martin Thornton sees the Cistercian invention of "lay brothers" in the twelfth century as a significant revolution: these men were fully monks, but their vocation was working on the land rather than singing in choir. The importance of this is that it recognizes the essential equality before God of two very different vocations: difference and hierarchy are both valid, and neither undermines the equality.

In the modern world, monasteries and convents have a much smaller place in the social order. But their unique place in a very highly differentiated society still has value, and they also serve, when they are doing their job, as a microcosm of the way that unity in diversity should work in the Christian life. Some are called to an explicit, full-time, visible Christian and monastic commitment; others, to some kind of "extended" relationship with that commitment; still others, to go about their Christian life without any such involvement. All may be equally responses to God's call, and so of equal value before God.

The hunger for this sort of community is very great today. Perhaps that is one reason why people visit convents and monasteries: they are seeking a place to belong. The ancient monastic work of hospitality has never been more needed, not because there are no "hotels" but because people are lonely. So simple a matter as publicizing that a monastic guest house *does* accept guests for Thanksgiving and Christmas seems to meet a surprisingly great need. Some of these people go on to look to the monastic community as a second family, or even as a primary one. They may not be in the least called to monastic life themselves, and certainly not to any long-term commitment to it. But by being Associates or even just friends and occasional guests of a religious house, they find that they have a place to belong. Being ready and able to respond to this new need is one way that religious communities have adapted to the changes in our culture.

If life as a whole is communal, so specifically is Christian prayer. The liturgical, biblical type of prayer we have discussed here is the prayer of a community. As we have seen, to pray the Psalms and the biblical story enables us both to enter into that Story and to be a part of the community that lives by it. For a Christian who feels alone and isolated, and who perhaps does his praying in a secular setting with little human support, this is a tremendously liberating and uplifting concept. We are indeed surrounded by a great cloud of witnesses, and we are called to be ourselves part of that cloud. My little prayer isn't worth much; but it both is the prayer of Christ himself and adds its little note to the one great chorus of praise.

II Praying the Lord's Prayer

Aconvent today attracts many people who ask, in one way or another, "How can I pray?" or "How can I pray better?" Some of these are already living lives well integrated into their local Christian communities and share regularly in the liturgy. Others say something like, "No, I don't go to church, but I'm really very *spiritual*." Almost all these inquirers are thinking of prayer exclusively as a purely private, individual activity. With the emphasis in today's culture on "experience" and "satisfaction," they are, quite understandably, looking for ways to "enrich" or "improve" their "experience" in this very private inner activity. What does the Gospel have to say to these earnest people? How can this sincere desire be integrated into the larger frame of the Christian story?

"One of [Jesus'] disciples said to him, 'Lord, teach us to pray, as John taught his disciples'" (Luke 11:1). These men also wanted to pray and knew that they did not know how. Jesus was obviously so close to God that surely he could teach them. Jesus replied to this request not by giving a theological discourse or a psychological analysis but by teaching them what has always been called the Lord's Prayer.

Our Father, who art in heaven, hallowed be thy Name. Thy Kingdom come, thy will be done, on earth as it is in heaven. Give us this day our daily bread. And forgive us our trespasses, as we forgive those who trespass against us. And lead us not into temptation, but deliver us from evil. For thine is the kingdom, and the power, and the glory, for ever and ever. Amen.

Many of us have been saying this prayer since childhood. Perhaps we think of it as an elementary or childish formula, something to outgrow, or as a rote repetition that has little to do with the "spiritual life." But the masters of that life say No, this prayer contains the essentials of all we need to know about Christian prayer, and to grow in prayer is to be able to pray it better. Several great Christian writers have written systematic expositions of the "Our Father," and these still have much to teach us. Much of what follows is based on Cyprian's commentary in the third century,[1] with additions from Origen and various other sources. Some writers lay considerable stress on the fact that Matthew and Luke give rather different texts, but most of them comment chiefly on the longer Matthean version. All emphasize that rote repetition is not the point. We do not outgrow saying this prayer that Jesus taught us, but we should continue to grow into the fullness of the Scripture's meaning. All teach also that our prayer from beginning to end is the work of grace. The words are given by God, and so is the spirit (and the Spirit) that enables us to pray. We are *bold* to say, "Our Father."

Our Father. We say "*Our* Father." The teacher of peace and master of unity does not want us to pray individually and privately in the sense of praying only for ourselves. We do not say "*My* Father" or "Give me my daily bread," nor do we seek forgiveness only for ourselves. Our prayer, even when we are alone, is public and in common; when we pray, we pray for the whole people, for we, the whole people, are one.

We say "Father" not by any natural right but because we belong to Christ, the only-begotten Son of God. The new man, born again and restored to God by grace, says first of all "Father" because he

---

1. One edition of *St. Cyprian on the Lord's Prayer* is that edited by T. Herbert Bundley (London: SPCK, 1914). Origen's teaching is contained in his work *On Prayer*.

has now begun to be a son. He who has believed in God's Name and has become a son of God ought at once to begin to give thanks and proclaim himself as such by declaring that he has a Father in heaven. Since Christ is the Son of God, and we are baptized into Christ, so may we call ourselves sons and daughters of God. We would not have dared to aspire to call God "Father" had not he himself commanded us so to pray. We ought then to realize that when we call God "Father," we ought to act as sons and daughters of God and as children pleasing to him.

These third-century thoughts of Saint Cyprian's may be especially valuable, and even countercultural, today. The "Our" stresses the corporate nature of all Christian life and prayer. However "private" my prayer may be — and that time with the door closed is essential to the Christian life — it is still a part of the prayer of the whole Church and a tiny piece of Christ's offering to the Father. The "Father" encapsulates the nature of our relationship with God. It is a friendship and a dialogue between persons, and a parent-child relationship in which God is very definitely the "senior partner." He is in charge, both in calling us to pray at all and in teaching us how to do so. This is the ground of reverence, respect, and obedience, as well as of personal trust and love.

Who art in heaven. Even in the third century, Cyprian knew that God is not somewhere "up there" on a throne. He tells us clearly that God is not limited by a bodily nature and does not dwell "in heaven" as a place. Rather, all things are contained and held together *in God*. That is why Paul can write, "Our citizenship is in heaven," because we are in God. As we come to realize this, our prayer will not be limited to the recital of set words at fixed times of prayer. As we learn to pray without ceasing, our whole life will say "Our Father, who art in heaven."

Hallowed be thy Name. We cannot "hallow" God, but we ask that his Name may be hallowed in us. The Lord himself says, "Be holy as I am holy." We must pray that, having been hallowed in baptism, we may persevere as we have begun. For this we must ask each day, for we fall daily and need daily purification.

Thy Kingdom come. God always rules, and there is no beginning and no end to his Kingdom. But we ask that God's rule be present *in us,* that the Kingdom of God should spring up and bear fruit and be perfected *in us.* Every sinner is under the tyranny of the Prince of this world. Paul bids us submit no longer to sin, which desires to reign over us; so we pray that God instead may reign in our lives. This is a prayer for the final Coming, but it is also a prayer for the daily increase of God's rule within our own hearts.

Thy will be done in heaven and in earth. (Cyprian quotes a text slightly different from the one we know.) We do not pray that God may do his own will, for who could prevent him? We do ask that we may be able to do what God wills. But we are opposed by the devil and held back by our own frailty and sin. So we must ask that God's will may be done in us, and that we may be enabled to choose and obey his will. Even the Lord, in the fullness of his human nature, says, "Father, if it be possible, let this cup pass from me. Nevertheless, not as I will, but as thou wilt" (Matt. 26:39). And Mary says to the angel Gabriel, "Be it unto me according to thy word" (Luke 1:38).

We pray that the will of God may be done both in heaven and in earth. We possess a body from earth and a spirit from heaven. We are ourselves in earth and in heaven, and in both, in body and in spirit, we pray that God's will may be done. If our citizenship is in heaven, and where God's will is done *is* heaven, then earth will not remain "earth," at least not fallen earth separated from God. C. S. Lewis comments here that *be done* is much stronger in English than in the Greek or Latin of the patristic writers. It suggests that there are things that need doing, and part of my prayer is to get up and start doing them. "Thy will be done — by me — now."[2]

Give us this day our daily bread. This may be understood both spiritually and literally. For Christ is the Bread of Life, and we pray that this Bread be given to us daily, that we who live and abide in Christ may not fall away from his Body. (Note that apparently daily Communion was thought quite normal in Saint Cyprian's time.) We also are taught to ask God to supply our bodily needs. We can understand further that we should ask only for what is really

2. C. S. Lewis, *Letters to Malcolm* (New York: Harcourt, Brace & World, 1963), p. 26.

necessary, and only for today's food, not for the future. The Greek word usually translated *daily* is *epiousion,* a rare word known only here. It may mean "necessary" or "for tomorrow." Some commentators have taken it to mean something like *supersubstantial,* which looks like a reasonable derivation but is probably false. The modern British writer Rose Macaulay comments, "I rather wish it did mean supersubstantial; it is perhaps a better meaning than daily, but apparently it doesn't. Still, in saying it one can think of spiritual food if one likes, of course."[3] It certainly is true that the devotional meaning of Scripture can rightly be much wider than the strictly scholarly interpretation. This becomes dishonest only if one then claims the extended devotional meaning as the literal and scholarly one.

Forgive us our debts as we also forgive our debtors. Unfortunately, as Lewis comments, not much exposition is needed here! We all fall daily and must daily ask pardon, so that we who are fed by God may continue to live in God. Thus our needs are provided, not only for temporal life but for the life that is eternal. And God clearly lays down the condition that we ourselves have forgiven our debtors. "I forgave you all that debt because you besought me; and should not you have had mercy on your fellow servant?" (Matt. 18:32-33).

Suffer us not to be led into temptation. The more familiar form of this clause causes difficulties for many people, because it sounds to them as if God would deliberately tempt us to do wrong. The contemporary translation "Save us from the time of trial" avoids that difficulty but is not what the Greek says. This is Cyprian's text, following Tertullian, and makes explicit the sense in which probably most of us understand it. In this version, we are taught that the Adversary can do nothing against us without God's permission. We are also warned against our own infirmity and weakness, lest any of us should insolently exalt ourselves. The Lord taught humility: "Watch and pray lest you enter into temptation" (Mark 14:38).

But deliver us from the Evil One. The Greek or the Latin can

---

3. Rose Macaulay, *Letters to a Friend, 1950-1952* (New York: Atheneum, 1962), p. 153.

mean either "evil" or "the Evil One." This includes everything that the Enemy may contrive against us in this world. We are safe and secure if we trust in God to deliver us when we pray. Nothing more remains; for what fear can he have of the world who has the eternal God for his protector?

For thine is the kingdom and the power and the glory. The older commentators do not include the doxology, because it is not found in most of the early Gospel texts. The Lord's Prayer, taken without it, ends with a prayer for protection, and this is certainly appropriate. If the doxology is added, it lifts up our hearts to contemplation of the eternal and unchanging Kingdom of God and provides an assurance that "All shall be well, and all manner of thing shall be well."

Reflections like these make it very clear that the Lord's Prayer is much more a way to live than a formula to recite. Distinguishing among "private prayer," corporate worship, and the rest of the Christian life is rather artificial, for all of these things are necessary, and all are interconnected. "Learning to pray" is just another name for "learning to be a Christian," and it runs into all the same difficulties.

There are, however, some basic principles of the life of "private prayer" that may be helpful. Many people have gotten the idea as children that "praying" simply means "asking God for what you want." If we remember that prayer is first of all *a relationship,* and a relationship within the life-and-death drama of the Christian Gospel, we will understand that a great deal more is involved. An analysis of the Lord's Prayer like the one in this chapter shows that this alone is a very full pattern for a Christian's prayers. As the old monk said to the young heroine of *Kristin Lavransdatter,* "You have not prayed until you have said your Paternoster without guile." Nevertheless, some other traditional guidelines may be useful. One outline lists five parts, or dimensions, which cover the whole field of "prayer." These are *Adoration* (worshiping God because he is God), *Thanksgiving, Confession* (or Contrition), *Intercession* (prayer for others), and, last, *Petition* (prayer for our own needs).

Some practical guidelines may also be in order. The only way to learn to pray is to pray, and to pray every day, whether one is in the mood or not. Many people find it helpful to set apart a definite daily time and a special place, marked with a crucifix or an icon or a picture. Cyprian gives advice on "how" to pray, telling us that our petitions should be disciplined, restrained, and modest: "The insolent man makes a great deal of noise; the modest man shows moderation even in prayer. The Lord teaches us to pray in private, in remote, hidden places." Even beginners in prayer may come up against puzzling experiences and great Christian mysteries much sooner than they might expect. Many excellent books have been written to help those who are learning to pray (C. S. Lewis's *Letters to Malcolm* is perhaps one of the best), and many people also seek guidance from a spiritual director.

Some day, please God, we will learn to live so closely with our God and Father that all of our life will be prayer, and we will move easily between time on our knees, time at work, and time with our friends, bringing all of these into our prayer. Meanwhile, the discipline of daily prayer, modeled on the Lord's own prayer, can help each of us to grow in loving friendship with the God who made and calls and loves us.

12 Whose Service Is Perfect Freedom

An earlier version of this chapter was addressed to the young people of St. Michael's Conference. Some references to that context have been retained.

This week in our chapel talks we have been examining the Lord's Prayer, the pattern Jesus gave us for all of our prayers. Tonight we have reached "Thy will be done." So we have to think about obedience, and specifically about Christian obedience. "Thy will, not mine, be done." If you can say this to God easily, then I suggest one of two things to you. Either you are very far along indeed on the path toward Christian holiness, or you've never thought very much about what you are saying. But for most of us, who do at least sometimes think about what we are saying, this can be a very hard prayer to pray. Let's think a little about what Christian obedience might mean, what we might be committing ourselves to when we pray this prayer.

The very word "obedience" frightens some people. This might be because they simply would rather have their way. But on another level, sometimes they might be frightened because they think that "to obey" means never to grow up, always to remain dependent on someone else, and never to take any responsibility. They think, and think rightly, that they *should* be taking responsibility. How can we understand "obedience" in a way that a responsible, thinking adult can accept? One of the collects in the Book of Common Prayer says of God, "His service is perfect freedom." This sounds paradoxical, and it is even more of a paradox in the original Latin: *cui servire est regnare* — "to be God's slave is to be a king." Like many other things in Christianity, this is indeed a paradox, and it is one worth thinking through quite carefully.

If you know any small children aged two or three, you may have noticed that a child of this age can be very sweet, but he is also very fond of the word "No." He — or, of course, she — is likely to be very fond of getting his own way, and rather likely to have a tantrum when he — or, of course, she — fails to get it; not always very fond of doing as he is told, of sitting still, of giving in to authority. In fact, left to himself, this child is likely to be a little savage, and somebody has got to housebreak him and give him some basic obedience training for his own good and for the survival of his family. Unfortunately, a few people never get that training and never grow out of this stage. In fact, they become grown-up spoiled brats, more formally called sociopaths, and many of them wind up either in jail or as self-centered, self-pitying adults with no friends — or both. Some kind of obedience, of accepting some control over yourself from outside, is absolutely necessary for survival in society. This is not yet Christian obedience; it's a long way from it. But it certainly is necessary. So one piece of obedience is learning to accept authority and to give up your own way.

Of course, this is only one side of the story. That spirit of independence, of self-assertion, of wanting "my way" that we see in the "terrible twos" isn't all bad. It's a very necessary part of a child's growing up, of establishing his own identity, of learning to take responsibility for his own life, of learning to make real choices. The rebellion, the exaggeration, and the selfishness are bad, and the child has to be taught his way out of them. But the stage is necessary. You young adults in this chapel today are going through a later and equally necessary stage of the same growth process: learning to make your own decisions, to take responsibility for your own lives and actions, to define your identity before God and before your peers. It's not always a simple or easy process, is it? And it is right and necessary and part of God's will for you that you should learn to have a mind and will of your own, to stand on your own two feet and to make responsible choices. Again, it is the selfishness and the rebellion that are wrong. So, whatever Christian obedience means, it does mean taking responsibility.

That idea — that being an adult Christian means taking responsibility — should help us to see what's wrong with one very dangerous sort of so-called obedience, a sort that gives the whole thing a bad name. This is the rag-doll sort, the "tell me what to do next, tell me what I want" sort. The sort that accepts blindly anything that anyone with any sort of "authority" says — from the expert quoted in a commercial to the demagogue who stirs up a crowd to riot. The sort that drives teachers wild (I speak from experience): "Tell me what I want to write a paper on"; "I know this is the wrong answer, but that's what you told me." The sort that will make a soldier or a policeman fire on a crowd of children because "authority" gave the command. This may be a kind of obedience, but it is most definitely not Christian obedience. It's laziness, and it's evasion of our own responsibility. God does not want limp rag-dolls with no backbone, and he does not want little tin soldiers. He may ask hard things of us, and sometimes seemingly unreasonable things of us, but he does not want blind, passive, irrational obedience. He wants grown-up people who can make free, adult, responsible, loving choices.

So what *does* it mean to say to the Lord God, "Thy will be done"? We have many examples in the Bible and in Christian history. Let's look briefly at the two greatest ones.

At the beginning of Luke's Gospel, the angel tells Mary that God wants her to be the mother of the Messiah, of his own Son, by the power of the Holy Spirit. What does Mary say in response? There are several things she could say, like "Who, me?" or "Please find someone else." But what does she say? She asks one question: "How shall this be?" The angel says, "Nothing is impossible with God," which means "The Holy Spirit can do this." And at this point Mary has a choice. She can obey, or she can refuse. She's standing at exactly the same spot where Eve was standing, with a moral choice to make. She knows what God wants, and she has to choose. Eve chose wrong. But what does Mary say? "Behold, the handmaid of the Lord" — that is, "I accept your will for me; I will cooperate; I will follow your plan." Is this going to be easy? Is it ever easy to be chosen for a big job? First she will have to tell Joseph — and her parents — that she is pregnant. Is that going to be simple? Then who knows what may come after this quite incalculable beginning? But she trusts God; she says to the angel, "Yes, I will cooperate. I trust you to make this work out for good and for the glory of God." And not long afterward she learns to sing, "My soul doth magnify the Lord."

The greatest example of all, of course, is Jesus' own example in the Garden of Gethsemane. He knows that he's about to be arrested, and he knows or is fairly sure that he's about to be executed, and that, humanly speaking, his life's mission is about to end in one resounding, crashing failure. Remember, he is also fully one with the Father, although we cannot perfectly understand what this means, and there is no rebellion in him. Does he have a choice? Yes, although this is a great mystery, he has a choice. Can he accept what is coming calmly and peacefully? No, he can't. No, by the great mercy of God, he can't, and his struggle to accept the Father's will has been recorded for us to strengthen us when we can't, either: "Father, if it be possible, let this cup pass from me. Nevertheless, not as I will, but as you will." We see what the struggle costs him; but we also see that the struggle ends in his *Fiat*, his praying of the prayer he taught us: "Thy will be done." He is saying, "I trust the Father; I will obey; I will follow whatever the cost. And I will believe that the end is good."

So what is involved when we, like our Lord Jesus Christ and like our Lady Saint Mary, pray to the Father, "Thy will be done"? We are making a choice, a responsible decision, and we are saying to God, "I trust the way you want to run your world, and I want to cooperate with it. I choose your way, even when I don't understand it, instead of my own self-centered way." This is an act of trust and an act of love. It's not just acquiescence: "Oh well, do it your way — I can't be bothered." It's not formal obedience covering up rebellion: "I'll do what you say, but I don't have to like it." It's a choice to choose God — and so it is one piece of our whole Christian discipleship. It's also a choice to trust God, to believe that what he wants really is good, really is best, really leads to the Kingdom — and that therefore it's what we really want too. It is not denying our own will but deliberately conforming our own will to a greater, wiser, and more loving will. There's a critical difference between these two things.

If we want to obey God, to do God's will, even to accept God's will, there are two steps involved. One is to find out what that will is, and the second is to choose that will with all the strength of our own will and with all the strength of God's grace.

The first of these is called *discernment*, and it involves using all of our faculties to find out and to understand what God is asking of us. Sometimes this is obvious. Sometimes it's clearly spelled out for us in the Bible, in the teaching we have received, in the circumstances God gives us. Sometimes it's a lot more subtle than that, and we really have to work and pray and study and consult. In little things we should be able to decide fairly easily, but in big things it may be important to go to some trouble. Many of you are at a point in your lives where big questions need to be discerned and answered. What should I study? Where? Should I go on to school or go directly to work now? Is God perhaps calling me to some form of full-time Christian service, perhaps to be a priest or a sister or a missionary, or does he want me to be a Christian doctor or accountant and/or parent? Two people may ask, Should we get married now? These big questions are worth much thought and prayer and the advice of those you trust. Once in a great while God seems to speak very directly, perhaps through the Bible or something someone says, perhaps in your own prayers. This kind of call can seem very certain. Even so, it may be a good idea to ask advice from someone you trust, because we can deceive ourselves very easily.

Sometimes the answer isn't so simple, and often the answer is unique and just for you, not the same as someone else's. Here's a particularly clear example. Two young men may pray earnestly for discernment about military service. One may become a career army officer, and the other may be called to be a conscientious objector, and both may be acting in good conscience, and neither may judge the other. We need wisdom here to distinguish between what we want and what we objectively think God wants. These are not always different, because he created us to want the good. If you really want something, that may mean God is speaking to you.

But the other side of this process is more important, and it is the same for all of us. Not only must we discern what God's will is, but we must choose to choose it. We must learn the difference between real Christian obedience and all that stubborn rebellion, that naughty, terrible-twos "I want my own way," and pray for the grace to want God's will, in love and trust and obedience, because we know he loves us. What do you *really* want? Do you want what is good, what is true, what is beautiful? Do you want to respond in love to God's love? Do you want to do what you know you *ought* to do? Do you at least want to want one of these things, whichever one speaks most strongly to you? (The good, the true, and the beautiful are really different names for the same thing.) Or do you want to please your little self-centered self? The way we learn to want God's will — or to want to want God's will — in love and trust is to pray, and to practice choosing, and to pray some more for the grace of conversion. This is why Jesus taught us to pray, every day, "Thy will be done" — not only so that his will can be done, but so that we can learn truly to want it.

In a few minutes, when we go to dinner, we will say the Angelus together and say with Mary, "Behold, the handmaid of the Lord. Be it unto me according to thy word." I have been saying this prayer every day for lo these many years, and I am still beginning to learn to pray this prayer. Sometimes it is easy, and sometimes it is very hard indeed. I have met some of those paradoxes I mentioned earlier. Sometimes the seemingly impossible thing God is asking turns out to be a blessing I could not have imagined, and God's "No" to something I wanted very much turns out to be a "Yes" to something even better. So I choose to go on praying to be able to choose God, and praying to be able to trust and obey him in love and in response to the love I know he has for me. I know that he wants the very best for all of us and will bring it into being if we obey — but it isn't always easy to see and accept this. And I pray that each of you may pray this prayer and grow in learning this way of obedience, as we follow the Lord whose service, as the collect says, is the only true and perfect freedom.

13 If Only . . .

Our Sister Juliana, who died some years ago, was an avid Scrabble player. She was also a bit of "everybody's grandmother," inclined to give uncomfortably apt advice on all occasions. She would be playing merrily along and would say, "Oh, if only I had an *e* or an *m*," or whatever it might be. "But you mustn't say *If only*. You can only play the letters you have."

Of course that adage applies, and Sister Juliana perfectly well meant to apply it, and to a lot more than a Scrabble game. "If only" I had a new car, or a better voice, or a week off, or more patience. . . . (Lord, give me patience, and I want it *right now*.) If only I had been born fifty years sooner, or later, or in a different family. If only the world weren't in such a mess. But this is the world God has put you in, these are the talents he has given you, and this is your task. You can only play the letters you have.

Wait a minute. There is, there really is, a use for *if only*. If only I knew more about accounting. . . . Maybe there's a course or a book. If only we had more room for guests. . . . Let's build. If only I could get along better with Jane. . . . Let's try a different tack. *If only* gives us a chance to dream, to explore, to open up new possibilities. Thinking in the subjunctive is a characteristically human thing to do, and it can be the first step to new discoveries and new achievements. So what's wrong with it? You can only play the letters you have; but maybe there are words you hadn't thought of, or maybe this is the time to scrap your letters and begin again from the beginning.

So, if your *if only* is a doorway to new possibilities, it is good and useful and may very well be from God. But if your *if only* is an excuse for doing nothing and is making you a chronic grouch, then beware, for this *if only* is from the Father of Lies. For all her good-natured fussing, Sister Juliana was a truly happy person, because she knew what to do with her *if only*. She played the letters she had. This is no new lesson; we've all heard it many times in various idioms. At its deepest, it is simply a translation into "homely" terms of a lesson we have from the Lord himself: "Father, if it be possible, let this cup pass from me. . . . Nevertheless, not as I will, but as thou wilt." Jesus played the letters he had, from the carpenter's home to the Cross, and by so doing he redeemed the world.

14 The Cloud of Witnesses:
The Story in Some Modern Lives

The Venerable Bede, a monk of Jarrow in the north of England in the eighth century, can well be called the father of English historians. His *History of the English Church and People* is the principal, and often the only, source we have for the period and the people he records. He recounts the stories of many saints of his own time, but his approach is not that of a modern biographer. In the life of a holy person he sees the pattern of the life of Christ:

> This pattern has been from the first century until today the life, death and resurrection of Jesus Christ. Christians are not called saints because they are interesting or brave, pious, just, well-behaved or great; they are saints insofar as they "put on Christ" (Gal. 3:27), "in whom dwells all the fulness of the Godhead" (Col. 2:9). . . . The question that Bede, like any hagiographer, asked is not: what school did this man go to? who were his friends and enemies? what were his hobbies? or what did he look like? but whether in this human life and death the marks of the Lord Jesus were visible.[1]

1. Sister Benedicta Ward, SLG, *The Venerable Bede* (Harrisburg, Pa.: Morehouse Publishing, 1990), p. 89.

It was Bede's style, and the fashion of his age, to be very explicit about this, and especially to dwell on the miracles that were the primary evidence for his subject's sanctity. Today we might prefer simply to tell the story and let it speak for itself. Nevertheless, like Bede, we *like* the stories of saints and heroes, and we can profit from hearing how the Christian pattern has been lived out in a variety of lives. This is certainly the biblical way, for both Old and New Testaments are full of people's stories. The pattern is always recognizable, the pattern of creation, rebellion, redemption, and the great goodness and love of God.

We can read this story in the Bible, from Genesis to Revelation; in the lives of Christians over many centuries; and often in our own lives and the lives of those around us. Yet God never repeats himself: Paul is not Peter, and a Saint Francis is very different from a Saint Teresa. Furthermore, the story needs to be retold for each new age. The men and women of God may exemplify this story in any of several ways. Some are noteworthy because they live the story in their own lives, some because they understand it clearly and can teach it, and still others because their imaginative vision can recreate the story in drama and fiction. Bede both lived the Christian story himself, quietly and faithfully in his monastery, and perceived and recorded it in the lives of others. The more we know of the lives and thoughts of our fellow Christians, the more we can see of the manifold wisdom of God. The notes that follow introduce a few examples, from among countless others, who may serve to illustrate the living out in concrete dailyness of the Gospel pattern. Most of these people are from the generation now just past (in fact, most of them knew each other), so that they do belong to our own time but are at a sufficient distance to be considered objectively.

Since his death in 1963, it has become increasingly clear that C. S. Lewis is one of the greatest evangelists and Christian apologists of our time. He, and the circle of friends who gathered around him at Oxford in the 1930s and 1940s, illustrate all three forms of the pattern. "Jack" Lewis, J. R. R. Tolkien, Charles Williams, and their lesser-known friends among the group called the Inklings were first of all living the Christian life themselves, in a modern university setting, and their own biographies are of interest for that reason.[2] Second, several of them wrote and taught orthodox Christian doctrine in forms that seem to be of lasting value. Lewis's *Mere Christianity* remains one of the best introductions to the Faith.[3] Third, all three of them were gifted with imaginations that expressed solid Christianity in attractive and very diverse forms: Lewis's Narnia chronicles and his science fiction, Tolkien's *Lord of the Rings,* and Williams's "thrillers."

The interactions among these Inklings and their friends are especially interesting. Many of their best writings were hammered out in long evening talkfests, being polished and improved by the criticism of other keen minds. The influence of both Tolkien and Williams certainly shows in Lewis's space trilogy; *That Hideous Strength* has been described as "a Charles Williams novel written by C. S. Lewis." Although T. S. Eliot was not an Inkling, he and Williams tossed "the still point of the turning world" back and forth like a tennis ball through a whole series of their writings.[4] Dorothy Sayers was not an Inkling, either — no woman was — but she contributed an important essay to *Essays Presented to Charles Williams,* edited by Lewis.

Another possible influence here does not seem to have been much noticed. Some of my generation grew up on the children's stories of Arthur Ransome, especially *Swallows and Amazons*[5] and its sequels. The Walker children in these stories bear a quite remarkable resemblance to the Pevensies of the Narnia books: John is a leader like Peter, Titty suggests the sensitive Lucy, and each family has a "sensible" Susan. Ransome does not deal with faerie; his world is neither Narnia nor Middle-earth, but simply the English Lake District. He writes not about large moral issues but about youngsters learning to camp and explore on their own. But he certainly lays a solid ground-

2. Humphrey Carpenter, *The Inklings* (Boston: Houghton Mifflin Co., 1979).

3. C. S. Lewis, *Mere Christianity* (New York: Macmillan, 1958).

4. Sebastian Knowles, *A Purgatorial Flame: Seven British Writers in the Second World War* (Philadelphia: University of Pennsylvania Press, 1990), p. 156. Knowles relates this to the Fool in Charles Williams's *Greater Trumps* and documents how the two authors batted the image back and forth. It appears first in Eliot's "Coriolan" in 1931. Then it "is passed from *The Greater Trumps* [1932], to *Burnt Norton* [1936], to *Descent into Hell* [1937], to *East Coker* [1940]."

5. Arthur Ransome, *Swallows and Amazons* (Philadelphia: Lippincott, 1931).

work for these larger issues. His children can be free-ranging pirates and ordinary children at the same time: "We would have given you broadside for broadside until one of us sank, even if it made us late for lunch." One wonders whether Ransome and Lewis knew each other and whether they shared their imaginative worlds.

Three other writers were not exactly a group, but all were novelists, and all, as it happens, were women. Rose Macaulay was roughly a contemporary of the Inklings but not part of their circle, though Lewis mentions meeting her. Her novel *The Towers of Trebizond*[6] is both a very funny Turkish travelogue and the rather wistful tale of a young woman who has somehow lost her dream city and is wondering how to find it again. This story turns out to echo the author's own. Her story is that of the Prodigal Daughter, with a happy ending. As a young writer living in London before the First World War, Rose was a devout Christian. Then she became involved in an affair with a married man that lasted for some years, until his death. She realized for herself that this relationship could not be combined with Christian practice, and she chose to abandon the Church rather than her lover. Much later she came to realize that this was putting second things first and had been profoundly wrong, no matter how lovely it had been at the time. She repented very deeply, made her confession, and became again a regular communicant. Her published letters, as well as the novel, reveal her as cultured, witty, profoundly sensitive to spiritual and moral questions, and humbly and gently pleased (and amused) at her honorary doctorate from Cambridge.

Like Miss Macaulay, Elizabeth Goudge made her entire life as a writer. The only child of an academic theologian, she never married, though she hints several times that she may have lost someone in World War I. Unlike Miss Macaulay, she traveled little and had rather limited contacts, and she was a faithful Anglican all her life. The characters in her novels are also, most of them, confined to a limited stage. Her autobiography, *The Joy of the Snow*,[7] makes clear how much of their

6. Rose Macaulay, *The Towers of Trebizond* (New York: Farrar, Straus & Cudahy, 1956).

7. Elizabeth Goudge, *The Joy of the Snow* (London: Hodder & Stoughton, 1974).

world is her own. Nevertheless, their very ordinary lives give them ample scope for deeply Christian dramas of pain, fidelity, forgiveness, and redemption. Several, like Miss Goudge herself, experience times of great suffering and darkness and learn to use these for the sake of others. Several of her male characters are deeply scarred by their experiences in the two world wars and find their way to forgiving and accepting forgiveness, and so to healing. The "Damerosehay" trilogy,[8] which focuses on the Eliot family, has especially fully developed characters, a strong sense of place, and a powerful treatment of the theme of fidelity. Some of her novels are historical: *The White Witch*[9] is a splendid account of the English Civil War. Not everyone likes this sort of novel or wants fiction as "semi-spiritual" reading, and some readers, apparently including Miss Macaulay, might find the author sometimes overly optimistic or sentimental. But others may find friends and fine twentieth-century Christian lives among her many works.

A third and slightly more recent writer may be more familiar in America. Ellis Peters's detective novels about Brother Cadfael[10] have become very popular and have also been televised to good effect. Here we have a faithful portrait of a twelfth-century English monastery and a likeable and very human hero-detective. The moral fiber of the stories is always sound, and sometimes the lesson is complex and very pointed. The people are very real, and good always triumphs, quite often in a new and reformed life for the miscreant.

Two modern Anglican theologians have already been quoted extensively in this book. Archbishop Michael Ramsey and Dr. Eric L. Mascall had a number of things in common. Both had roots in Cambridge; both were, by choice, dons; both wrote and taught extensively the same orthodox Anglo-Catholic theology, with a mind open to the contemporary world, and with a sense of

8. Elizabeth Goudge, *The Bird in the Tree* (London: Hodder & Stoughton, 1967); *Pilgrim's Inn* (New York: Coward-McCann, Inc., 1948), first published in England as *The Herb of Grace*; and *The Heart of the Family* (New York: Coward-McCann, Inc., 1953).

9. Elizabeth Goudge, *The White Witch* (New York: Coward-McCann, Inc., 1958).

10. Ellis Peters, *The Leper of Saint Giles* (London: Futura, 1984), and other titles. Other editions of this series are available.

humor. Neither originally intended an ecclesiastical career. Ramsey began as a promising and rather eccentric Liberal politician, Mascall as a mathematician, until he chose "not angles but angels." The differences are interesting. Ramsey made his mark young, with *The Gospel and the Catholic Church,* and refused many academic and ecclesiastical offers before he finally found himself a bishop and then an archbishop. He later said that one of the hardest decisions he ever made was to leave his Cambridge professorship when he was asked to become Bishop of Durham. But the young Liberal politician came to life again in the Archbishop of Canterbury, for he did not hesitate to take strong, public, and sometimes unpopular stands on issues like race relations and immigration. Mascall never had any ecclesiastical preferment at all, except a canonry in Truro; he was several times refused posts at his own university; and he wondered for extensive periods whether God, or anyone else, wanted him to do anything at all. Mascall was celibate and a member of the Oratory of the Good Shepherd; Ramsey married very happily. Both men published extensively, and both are the subjects of interesting biographies.[11] Mascall's "autobiography," he emphasizes, is not that, but a memoir. Characteristically, it is about "what he remembers," not about himself. A sure sign of sanctity is that he can laugh at himself:

The Owl, who has enormous eyes,
In consequence is very wise.
The Guinea-pig, whose eyes are small,
Has no intelligence at all.
Good Dr. Mascall's soulful eyes
Are intermediate in size,
And so he is, as you'd expect,
Of mediocre intellect.[12]

11. Owen Chadwick, *Michael Ramsey: A Life* (Oxford: Clarendon Press, 1990); James B. Simpson, *The Hundredth Archbishop of Canterbury* (New York: Harper & Row, 1962); Eric L. Mascall, *Saraband: The Memoirs of E. L. Mascall* (Leominster: Gracewing, 1992).
12. E. L. Mascall, *Pi in the High* (London: The Faith Press, 1959), p. 18.

The last "life" to be considered here is not of our own time at all and is entirely fictional. Sigrid Undset's novel *Kristin Lavransdatter*[13] might well have frightened me off as a teenager and a new Christian. It is set in fourteenth-century Norway, has been translated into somewhat archaic English, and is a thousand pages long. But I could not put it down then, and have since returned to it several times. The people, Kristin and her family, are fully alive, and their world is vividly depicted. More important, this was my first real look at a world where God and his will and his Church mattered supremely. Kristin is perhaps an "ordinary" woman: she grows up, marries, raises her family, and dies fairly young. Yet she learns, gradually, what it means to belong to God, to make choices, to sin and repent, to live out a commitment, and at last to lay down her life for another. *Pactum serva:* keep thy troth. This novel did not *make* me a Christian, but it certainly did as much as any one book to make me begin to grow as one. It is only one of countless biographies, real and fictional, that portray the Story of Jesus Christ and his Gospel lived out in the circumstances of one human life. This is the path to which all Christians are called.

13. Sigrid Undset, *Kristin Lavransdatter* (New York: Alfred A. Knopf, 1929; reprint, New York: Vintage Books, 1987).

15 Glory Be to God for Monday Morning: A Canticle for Ordinary Seasons

The angels were gone away from them into heaven:
 and the shepherds were left with their silly, bleating sheep.
When they came down from the mountain,
  Jesus was found alone,
 and the disciples wondered if they had dreamt the glory.
While they beheld, he was taken up, and a cloud received him
  out of their sight:
 "Go into Galilee, for there you shall see me."
The high and lofty One, who inhabiteth eternity,
 has pitched his tent and dwelt among us.
  Glory be to God for Monday morning.

It was a wonderful, exalted retreat, so *inspiring;*
 now it's commuter traffic, the kids, and the dirty laundry.
I just love to pray in the quiet early morning;
 why does the phone always have to ring?
When you pray, enter into your chamber and shut the door;
 Go ye into all the world and proclaim the Gospel.
Lord, if thou bidd'st us leave the mount,
 go with us to the plain.
  Glory be to God for Monday morning.

Bibliography

Abbott, Edwin. *Flatland,* with a foreword by Isaac Asimov. New York: Harper & Row–Perennial Library, 1984. (This book was first published in 1884.)

Augustine. *Confessions.* Translated and edited by John K. Ryan. Garden City, N.Y.: Doubleday–Image Books, 1960.

Benson, R. M. *The War Songs of the Prince of Peace.* Vol. 2. New York: E. P. Dutton & Co., 1901.

The Book of Common Prayer. New York: Oxford University Press, 1979.

Brooke, Avery. *Finding God in the World: Reflections on a Spiritual Journey.* Cambridge, Mass.: Cowley Publications, 1994.

Bundley, T. Herbert, ed. *St. Cyprian on the Lord's Prayer.* London: SPCK, 1914.

Caldecott, Stratford. "Speaking the Truths Only the Imagination May Grasp." *Touchstone* 11:5 (Sept./Oct. 1998): 44ff.

Carpenter, Humphrey. *The Inklings.* Boston: Houghton Mifflin Co., 1979.

Casserley, J. V. Langmead. *Christian Community.* London: Longmans, Green & Co., 1960.

Chadwick, Owen. *Michael Ramsey: A Life.* Oxford: Clarendon Press, 1990.

CR Quarterly, published by the Community of the Resurrection, Mirfield, West Yorkshire, WF14 OBN, England.

Daniélou, Jean, S.J., ed. *From Glory to Glory.* Translated and edited by Herbert Musurillo, S.J. New York: Charles Scribner's Sons, 1961.

Dix, Dom Gregory. *The Shape of the Liturgy*. Westminster, Eng.: The Dacre Press, 1943.

Goudge, Elizabeth. *The Bird in the Tree*. London: Hodder & Stoughton, 1967.

————. *The Heart of the Family*. New York: Coward-McCann, Inc., 1953.

————. *The Joy of the Snow*. London: Hodder & Stoughton, 1974.

————. *Pilgrim's Inn*. New York: Coward-McCann, Inc., 1948. (This book was first published in England as *The Herb of Grace*.)

————. *The White Witch*. New York: Coward-McCann, Inc., 1958.

Green, Roger Lancelyn, and Walter Hooper. *C. S. Lewis: A Biography*. New York and London: Harcourt Brace Jovanovich, 1974.

Hebert, A. G. *Liturgy and Society*. London: Faber & Faber, 1935.

Hick, John. *The Metaphor of God Incarnate: Christology in a Pluralistic Age*. Louisville: Westminster/John Knox Press, 1993.

Jenson, Robert W. "How the World Lost Its Story." *First Things* 36 (October 1993): 19-24.

Knowles, Sebastian. *A Purgatorial Flame: Seven British Writers in the Second World War*. Philadelphia: University of Pennsylvania Press, 1990.

Lewis, C. S. *Letters to Malcolm*. New York: Harcourt, Brace & World, 1963.

————. *Mere Christianity*. New York: Macmillan, 1958.

————. *Out of the Silent Planet*. New York: Macmillan, 1944.

————. *Perelandra*. New York: Macmillan, 1944.

————. *The Screwtape Letters*. New York: Macmillan, 1961.

————. *That Hideous Strength*. New York: Macmillan, 1946.

Macaulay, Rose. *Letters to a Friend, 1950-1952*. New York: Atheneum, 1962.

————. *The Towers of Trebizond*. New York: Farrar, Straus & Cudahy, 1956.

Mascall, Eric L. *Christ, the Christian, and the Church*. London: Longmans, Green & Co., 1946.

————. *Christian Theology and Natural Science*. London: Longmans, Green & Co., 1956.

————. *Corpus Christi*. London: Longmans, Green & Co., 1953.

————. *Pi in the High*. London: The Faith Press, 1959.

————. *The Recovery of Unity*. London: Longmans, Green & Co., 1958.

————. *Saraband: The Memoirs of E. L. Mascall*. Leominster: Gracewing, 1992.

Menzies, Lucy, ed. *Retreat Addresses of Edward Keble Talbot*. London: SPCK, 1954.

Mickelsen, A. Berkeley. *Interpreting the Bible.* Grand Rapids: Wm. B. Eerd-
    mans, 1963.

Mills, David, ed. "The Books that Form Souls." *The Evangelical Catholic* 17:3
    (May-June 1995).

————. *The Pilgrim's Guide: C. S. Lewis and the Art of Witness.* Grand Rapids:
    Wm. B. Eerdmans, 1998.

The Monastic Diurnal Revised. Peekskill, N.Y.: The Community of St. Mary,
    Eastern Province, 1989.

Mosley, Nicholas. *The Life of Raymond Raynes.* London: The Faith Press,
    1961.

Peters, Ellis. *The Leper of St. Giles.* London: Futura, 1984.

————. *Monk's Hood.* London: Futura Publications, 1984.

————. *The Virgin in the Ice.* London: Futural Publications, 1984.

Ramsey, Arthur Michael. *The Gospel and the Catholic Church.* London:
    Longmans, Green & Co., 1936. Reprint, Cambridge, Mass.: Cowley
    Publications, 1990.

Ransome, Arthur. *Swallows and Amazons.* Philadelphia: Lippincott, 1931.

Simpson, James B. *The Hundredth Archbishop of Canterbury.* New York:
    Harper & Row, 1962.

Sister Mary Hilary, CSM. *Ten Decades of Praise.* Racine, Wis.: DeKoven Foun-
    dation, 1965.

Thornton, Martin. *Pastoral Theology: A Reorientation.* London: SPCK, 1958.

Undset, Sigrid. *Kristin Lavransdatter.* New York: Alfred A. Knopf, 1929. Re-
    print, New York: Vintage Books, 1987.

Ward, Sister Benedicta, SLG. *The Venerable Bede.* Harrisburg, Pa.:
    Morehouse Publishing, 1990.

Wilkinson, Alan. *The Community of the Resurrection: A Centenary History.* Lon-
    don: SCM Press Ltd., 1992.